91

TOM PETERS
ESSENTIALS
LEADERSHIP

!
.

LONDON, NEW YORK, MUNICH,
MELBOURNE, AND DELHI

Editor **Michael Slind**
Project Art Editor **Jason Godfrey at Godfrey Design**
Senior Editor **Dawn Henderson**
DTP Design and Reproduction **Adam Walker**
Production Controller **Luca Frassinetti**
Managing Editor **Julie Oughton**
Managing Art Editor **Heather McCarry**
Publishing Manager **Adèle Hayward**
Category Publisher **Stephanie Jackson**
Art Director **Peter Luff**

First published in the USA in 2005 by
DK Publishing, Inc.
375 Hudson Street, New York, NY 10014

First published in Great Britain in 2005 by
Dorling Kindersley Limited,
80 Strand, London WC2R 0RL
A Penguin Company

2 4 6 8 10 9 7 5 3 1

DK books are available at special discounts for bulk purchases for sales promotions,
premiums, fund-raising, or educational use. For details contact: SpecialSales@dk.com

A Cataloging-in-Publication record for this book
is available from the Library of Congress.
(US) ISBN 0-7566-1055-9

A CIP catalog record for this book
is available from the British Library.
(UK) ISBN 1 4053 0257 7

Reproduced by Colourscan, Singapore
Printed and bound in China by South China Printing Company

Discover more at
www.dk.com

CONTENTS

INTRODUCTION

Re-imagining ... What's Essential

Fall 2003. I publish my Big Book ... *Business Excellence in a Disruptive Age*. It is, since the publication of *In Search of Excellence* in 1982, my most ambitious attempt to state comprehensively ... What Business Is. (Or Could Be.) (Or *Must* Be.)

The year following, 2004. While traveling to promote the book ... and while keeping up with my usual speaking and consulting schedule... I note a steadily increasing drumbeat. A drumbeat of consternation around the issue of "outsourcing." (Or "off-shoring.") Jobs going to India. Or China. Or just ... Somewhere Else.

What is to be done? How can people cope ... with the specter of ... massive job shrinkage? My (nutshell) answer: Job shrinkage is inevitable. Whether because of outsourcing or automation (which, long-term, may be a bigger deal than outsourcing), you can't count on any job being "there for you." What you can do is find ways to move yourself and your company Up the Value Chain ... and into the heart and soul of the New Economy.

Summer 2005. I publish a series of four quick and to-the-point books, one of which you now hold in your hand. The "Essentials" is what the series is called. As in: Here are the essential things you *must* know ... as you strive to *act* ... in this unstable, up-tempo, outsourcing-addled, out-of-this-world age.

New Economy, New Mandate, New Story

A lot of yogurt has hit the fan. In the near term, globalization continues to be a mixed blessing—a worthy end point, but messy and uneven to the extreme in its immediate impact. Waves of technological change engulf us—and confuse us. Corporate scandals erupt. Once-mighty titans (namely: big companies and the CEOs who lead them) fall from their lofty perches

And yet ... there *is* a New Economy.

Would you change places with your grandfather? Would you want to work 11 brutal hours a day ... in yesterday's Bethlehem Steel mill, or a Ford Motor Company factory circa 1935? Not me. Nor would I change places with my father ... who labored in a white-collar sweatshop, at the same company, in the same building, for 41 l-o-n-g years.

A workplace revolution is under way. No sensible person expects to spend a lifetime in a single corporation anymore. Some call this shift the "end of corporate responsibility." I call it ... the Beginning of Renewed Individual Responsibility. An extraordinary opportunity to take charge of our own lives.

Put me in charge! Make me Chairman and CEO and President and COO of Tom Inc.

That's what I ask! (Beg, in fact.)

I *love* business at its best. When it aims to foster growth and deliver exciting services to its clients and exciting opportunities to its employees. I especially *love* business at this moment of flux. This truly magical, albeit in many ways terrifying, moment.

I'm no Pollyanna. I've been around. (And then around.) My rose-colored glasses were long ago ground to powder by brutal reality.

Yet I am hopeful. Not hopeful that human beings will become more benign ... or that evil will evaporate ... or that greed will be regulated out of existence. But I am hopeful that in the New Economy people will see the power that comes from taking responsibility for their professional lives. And I am hopeful that they also will find pleasure in unleashing their instinctive curiosity and creativity.

The harsh news: This is Not Optional. The microchip will colonize all rote activities. And we will have to scramble to reinvent ourselves—as we did when we came off the farm and went into the factory, and then as we were ejected from the factory and delivered to the white-collar towers.

The exciting news (as I see it, anyway): This is Not Optional. The reinvented *you* and the reinvented *me* will have no choice but to scramble and add value in some meaningful way.

The Back-Story: A Tale/Trail of Disruption

Each book in the series builds on a central premise—the same premise that I propounded in the early chapters of *Re-imagine*! Herewith, an Executive Summary of that Progression of Ideas.

1. All bets are off. It is the foremost task—and responsibility—of our generation to re-imagine our enterprises and institutions, public and private. Rather strong rhetoric. But I believe it. The fundamental nature of the change now in progress has caught us off-stride and on our heels. No aspect of the way our institutions operate can be allowed to go unexamined. Or unchanged.

2. We are in a ... Brawl with No Rules. Business, politics, and, indeed, the essential nature of human interchange have come unglued. We have to make things up as we go along. (Success = SAV = "Screw Around Vigorously.") ("Fail. Forward. Fast.") Yesterday's strictures and structures leave us laughably—and tragically—unprepared for this Brawl with No Rules. From al Qaeda to Wal*Mart, new entrants on the world stage have flummoxed regnant institutions and their leaders.

3. Incrementalism is *Out*. Destruction is *In*. "Continuous improvement," the lead mantra of 1980s management, is now downright dangerous. All or nothing. ("Control. Alt. Delete.") We must gut the innards of our enterprises before new competitors do it for us—and to us.

4. InfoTech changes everything. There is no higher priority than the Total Transformation of all business practice to e-business practice. The new technologies are ... The Real Thing. The IT Revolution is in its infancy. And yet it has already changed the rules—changed them so fundamentally that years and years will pass before we can begin talking about constructing a new rule book.

5. Ninety percent of white-collar jobs as we know them (and, ultimately, 90 percent of all jobs as we know them) will be disemboweled in the next 15 years. Done. Gone. Kaput. Between the microprocessor, 60/60/24/7 connectivity, and outsourcing to developing countries, the developed nations' white-collar jobs are ... doomed. Time frame? Zero to 15 or 20 years. How confident am I on this point? Totally.

6. "Winners" (survivors!) will become *de facto* bosses of Me Inc. Self-reliance will, of necessity, replace corporate cosseting. Old-style corporate security is evaporating. Upshot: Free the cubicle slaves! The only defense is a good offense! Hackneyed? Sure. But no less true for being so. A scary ... but also immensely exciting ... New Age of Self-Reliance is being birthed before our eyes. Hurray!

Story Time—for a Storied Time

Building on that premise, each book in this series tells a story—a saga of how we will survive (and, perhaps, go beyond survival) in this Dizzy, Disruptive Age.

A Story about *Leadership*. Command-and-control management ... "leadership" from on high ... is obsolete. New Leadership draws on a new skill set—the hallmarks of which are improvisation and inspiration. It taps into the unique leadership attributes of women. It cultivates Great Talent by creating a Great Place to Work.

A Story about *Design*. New Value-Added derives less and less from "product" or "service" quality, and more and more from ... Something More. Something called "Experiences." Something called "Branding." Something called "Design."

A Story about *Talent*. It's a Brand You World. "Lifetime employment" at a corporation (aka "cubicle slavery") is out. Lifetime self-reinvention is in. The only fool-proof source of job security is ... your talent. And your talent will express itself by building a scintillating portfolio of WOW Projects and by Thinking Weird (as these weird, wild times demand).

A Story about *Trends*. Where, amid so much flux and discontinuity, are the Big Market Opportunities? They are hiding in plain sight. Go where they buyers are and where the money is—among women and among aging boomers.

The Story Re-imagined: What's New

To tell these stories, I have adapted selected chapters from *Re-imagine!* As necessary or as I've seen fit, I have nipped and tucked and otherwise revised each chapter throughout. Plus, I have salted the tale here and there with new supporting material.

In addition, I—along with the folks at my publisher, Dorling Kindersley—have re-imagined the the look-and-feel of each book from the inside-out. With *Re-imagine!*, we set out to re-invent the business book. We wanted to tell the story of a world of enterprise that is bursting at the seams with revolutionary possibility, and so we created a book that bursts forth with Passion and Energy and Color. For the Essentials series, we have retained those qualities, but we have also stripped the design of these books down to its ... essentials. Same Passion. Same Energy. Same Color. All in a format that fits in your hand ... and meets (we believe) your essential needs.

Two new features punctuate and amplify the Story Being Told.

First, capping each chapter is a list of "Top 10 To-Dos"—a one-page digest of the chapter in the form of action items that will inspire you to Do Something ... right away. Here again, the emphasis is on drilling down to ... what's essential.

Second, between certain chapters we include highlights from interviews with "Cool Friends"—smart people whose work has helped make me smarter. Their voices add insights that give texture to the story. Full-text versions of these and other interviews appear on my Web site (www.tompeters.com).

Last Words …

I don't expect you'll agree with everything that I say in this book. But I hope that when you disagree … you will disagree *angrily*. That you will be so pissed off that you'll … Do Something.

DOING SOMETHING. That's the essential idea, isn't it? The moral of my story—the story of What's Essential about the present moment in business—comes in the form of a tombstone. It's a tombstone that bears the epitaph that I most hope to avoid. To wit:

𝔗𝔥𝔬𝔪𝔞𝔰 𝔍. 𝔓𝔢𝔱𝔢𝔯𝔰
1942–𝔚𝔥𝔢𝔫𝔢𝔳𝔢𝔯
𝔥𝔢 𝔴𝔬𝔲𝔩𝔡 𝔥𝔞𝔳𝔢 𝔡𝔬𝔫𝔢 𝔰𝔬𝔪𝔢 𝔯𝔢𝔞𝔩𝔩𝔶 𝔠𝔬𝔬𝔩 𝔰𝔱𝔲𝔣𝔣 …
𝔟𝔲𝔱 𝔥𝔦𝔰 𝔟𝔬𝔰𝔰 𝔴𝔬𝔲𝔩𝔡𝔫'𝔱 𝔩𝔢𝔱 𝔥𝔦𝔪

Meanwhile, I know exactly how I *do* want my tombstone to read:

𝔗𝔥𝔬𝔪𝔞𝔰 𝔍. 𝔓𝔢𝔱𝔢𝔯𝔰
1942–𝔚𝔥𝔢𝔫𝔢𝔳𝔢𝔯
𝔥𝔢 𝔴𝔞𝔰 𝔞 𝔭𝔩𝔞𝔶𝔢𝔯!

Not "He got rich." Not "He became famous." Not even "He got things right." Rather: "He was a player." In other words: He did *not* sit on the sidelines … and watch the world go by … as it was undergoing the most profound shift of basic premises in the last several hundred years (if not the last thousand years).

Agree or disagree with me on anything else, but if you have a grain of integrity or spirit or spunk or verve or nerve, you must agree with me on this: Getting off the sidelines—Being a Player—is Not Optional.

No. In fact, Being a Player is … *Essential!*

1

PURSUING EXCELLENCE IN A DISRUPTIVE AGE: THE LEADERSHIP50

Contrasts

Was	Is
"Changing" people	Charging people up
Command and control	Creation of "context"
Think big thoughts	Do bold deeds
Plan, plan, plan	Play, play, play
Serenely aloof	Stubbornly angry
Purity	Paradox
"I don't care" ("... what you think")	"I don't know" ("... all the answers")
"Transforming" people	Transferring opportunity
Doing it all	Delegating
Smoke & mirrors (leadership as mystique)	Nuts & bolts (leadership as mastery)
The "plan clan"	The "action faction"
Worrying about one's image	Working one's imagination
Pure logic	Prosaic logistics
"Correcting" people	Connecting people
Leader as "wise man" (forget women)	Leader as "whys man" (or "woman"!)
Presiding	Pushing
Leading for ... the long haul	Leading with ... a long shot
Making a "killing"	Making a mark

!Rant

We are not prepared ...

We fall back, in these **CRAZY AND CHAOTIC TIMES**, on the command-and-control model of leadership—**a model that no longer accords with how dynamic leaders actually operate.**

WE SEEK SHELTER IN THE FANTASY OF A LEADER WHO HAS THE ANSWERS ... who promises "change" or "success" or "profits" in exchange for patient "followership" (aka "obedience"). • But in an age when all value flows from creativity and initiative, **we must imagine and embrace a model of leadership that is loose, open, and perpetually innovative.**

We ask leaders to be "good stewards" of the assets they inherit. • But in an age where **PERMANENCE IS A DANGEROUS DELUSION**, we must instead ask leaders to challenge the legacies they have inherited, **create entirely new value propositions—and then to get out before they get stale.**

!Vision

I imagine ...

A young woman, aged 27, who espies **A WONDROUS OPPORTUNITY TO RE-INVENT** her company's chronically creaky customer-service operation. • **She tells everyone she meets about this exciting inkling, and everyone says, "Great idea, but good luck!"** • Even so, she works (and works) (and works) the problem ... and eventually cobbles together a six-person project team. • **FANATICS ALL.** • The team includes a Talent Developer and a Profit Mechanic; our SuperWoman is Visionary and the Head Cheerleader. • Leading her team on a Voyage of Mutual Discovery, she finds out that her original notion wasn't quite right ... **but the unbounded quest ultimately results in something ... much, much stranger and far, far better.**

The Lead

Lead-Off Matter (A Muscular Definition)

Leadership is ... *Joyous!* It's a matchless opportunity to Make a Difference by marshaling the talents of others to a ... Seriously Cool Cause.

Leadership is ... *Horrible!* It's an exercise in sorting through the mess of human relations, in all their gory detail, day after day. (After day.)

Leadership is ... *Cool!* It's a Glorious Adventure that enables us to magnify our impact on the world.

Leadership is ... *Lonely!* It's a battle against doubt and dread in which you have only your own judgment about human nature to fall back on.

Leadership is ... *Different!* It's a matter not of "doing" excellence but of "inspiring" excellence in others.

Leadership is ... *The Ultimate Responsibility!* It's an assumption of accountability ... for people you cannot control, for actions that you do not perform, for institutions that may not share your deep and abiding sense of accountability.

Leadership is ... *not what you think!* It's not about "command and control" or kingly charisma. It's about living in the depths (flourishing in the chess game of big egos and big institutions) and soaring to the heights (rallying others to invent and then pursue seemingly impossible dreams).

Leadership is ... *The Ultimate New Mandate!* It's an apt prism through which to summarize this long journey that we have taken through our Disruptive Age. It's a never-ending project with a breathtakingly simple (and breathtakingly difficult) core objective: Re-imagine!

Leadership is ... **50 ideas.**

ership50

PREMISE: A LEADER'S LIMITS

1. Leaders Create Opportunities.

I was reading a newsletter from an educational organization (one that I support, incidentally). The title of the lead article sent me into ... an Immense Rage. It suggested that excellent (educational) institutions "transform people."

Nonsense!

Nobody "transforms" anybody else!

Instead, we create *opportunities* for people ... and then encourage them to apply their latent talents to grasp those opportunities.

The difference between those two notions is as subtle as ... A TRAIN GRANDE VITESSE COMING TOWARD YOU AT 115 MILES AN HOUR.

Leaders do *NOT* ... "transform people." Leaders instead construct a context in which ... *Voyages of Mutual Discovery* ... can take place.

Leaders provide access to a luxuriant portfolio of projects. Projects that challenge people to express their Innate Curiosity and to visit (or, indeed, to create) places that they (*and their*

leadership

the leadership50

leaders) had never dreamed of. And when the voyage bears fruit, leaders applaud like hell, stage "photo ops," and ring the church bells 100 times to commemorate the bravery of their "followers'" explorations!

TERMS LIMIT

I hate the terms "organizational change," "empowerment," and "motivation." We don't "change" people (or organizations). We don't "empower" people (or organizations). We don't "motivate" people (or organizations).

Scrap those terms. Stomp on them. Every one of them.

At the risk of sounding too much like Tony Robbins, I say: We awaken the latent talent already within those who work with (or for) us … by providing opportunities that justify their choosing to invest in us their most precious resources: their time and their emotional commitment.

"Places Never Dreamed Of." That is the heart of the matter: NO ONE HAS A CLUE!

BOSS = DOESN'T HAVE A CLUE.

FOLLOWER = DOESN'T HAVE A CLUE.

We must … discover-invent places that have not heretofore existed. (IT'S THE WHOLE DAMN POINT!) And if you don't have the … NERVE … to Encourage People … to Redraw the Map (or to Create a New Map) … well, then … YOU SHOULD NOT BE LEADING. ANYONE. ANYWHERE.

2. Leaders Say "I Don't Know."

For a leader, three words matter above all others. Those words, according to management guru-of-gurus Karl Weick: "*I DON'T KNOW.*"

"I don't know" is … the ALL-TIME PERMISSION SLIP. "I don't know" means: "Hey, *you* figure it out."

Karl explains: "The leader who says 'I don't know'

EXULTANT CONSULTANT

Leaders create projects. Great Leaders create … Awesome Quests.

Personal story: I reported to work as a McKinsey consultant in December 1974. Arrived at 8:30 a.m. Had keys by 10 a.m., an assignment by 11 a.m., a plane ticket by noon. Off to Calgary by 2 p.m.—to scope out demand and supply in the Canadian agrichemical business (by myself).

Within 5.5 hours, that is, I was pursuing my first of many … Quests.

I was scared to death. I was exultant.

essentially says that the group is facing a new ballgame where the old tools of logic may be its undoing rather than its salvation. To drop these tools is not to give up on finding a workable answer. It is only to give up on one means of answering that is ill-suited to the unstable, the unknowable, the unpredictable. To drop the heavy tools of rationality is to gain access to lightness in the form of intuitions, feelings, stories, experience, active listening, shared humanity, awareness in the moment, capability for fascination, awe, novel words, and empathy."

I DON'T KNOW

The "textbook" idea of leadership: Leader knows all! Leader gives orders! Followers follow! But in weird, wild, textbook-defiant times like these, the model of leader as "all-knowing commander and order-giver extraordinaire" is fatally and fundamentally flawed.

Leaders resort to the Command and Control model when they are … *scared*. That is: *scared as hell that followers will figure out that they (the leaders) don't have a clue as to what-the-hell-is-going-on.*

The Big Trick is turning "I don't know" into a show of strength, rather than an acknowledgment of weakness. Leaders *do* have a "weakness": They really *don't* "know." But what leaders offer isn't knowledge—it's a smidgen of wisdom and (above all) spirit. The spirit that goes into having the raw nerve to unleash the passion and unleash the talent of others. In fact, that's the ultimate "toughness" of leadership.

"HARD" TIME

Note well: This is not *a "soft" idea. This is a quintessentially hard business idea. The subtext of "I don't know" is: "We are Venturing into the Unknown. I hired you for a reason, and it wasn't to 'follow orders.' So figure something out. Make it up as you go along. And … damn well don't come home empty-handed."*

3. Leaders Are Rarely the Best Performers.

A symphony conductor is usually a good musician, but seldom a world-class performer. The most effective university deans are often *not* the best professors. The ability to lead … to Engage Others and to Turn Them On … rarely coincides with being at the tip-top of the … Individual Performance Heap.

Which is not to say that leaders shouldn't have a fingertip familiarity with their particular line of business. But the factors that make you good at the "people stuff" and the "inspiration stuff" and the "profit-making stuff" are quite distinct from the factors that vault you to the Pinnacle of Individual Mastery.

In business, alas, it's all too common to promote the "best" practitioner to the job of leading other practitioners. The best trainer becomes head of the training department. The best account manager becomes head of the sales department. And so on. Tellingly, that's not how things work in … True Talent Enterprises. (A symphony orchestra. A baseball team.) So why do we go that route in business? Beats me. Gross stupidity? Maybe. But more likely: a refusal to see that leadership is … a discrete, limited, special quality.

4. Leaders Are Talent Developers (Type I Leadership).

Great leaders on snorting steeds are important—but great talent developers are the bedrock of organizations that perform over the long haul.

Talent Development … is a 25/8/53 activity. And an OBSESSION … for those who would Truly Create a Legacy of Greatness. Jack Welch didn't have a "vision" at GE. Jack was the Premier Talent Developer of our times. Some people get their Ultimate Jollies out of … Developing Extraordinary Talent. (Their Hall of Fame hires are their Ultimate Bragging Rights.) Alas, some people don't. Even though we may call this group "leaders," they are fearful of hiring people who are better than they are, fearful of true diversity, fearful of odd ducks and rabble rousers.

5. Leaders Are Visionaries (Type II Leadership).

Two pieces of "art" hang on my writing-room wall in Vermont. Both are covers from *Life* magazine. The first cover shows Franklin Delano Roosevelt in 1933, in the pits of the Global Depression. The second cover features Winston Churchill in 1940, in the midst of the awful Battle of Britain.

The experts say Roosevelt was not much of an economist. And that Churchill was a questionable talent as military strategist. Yet they kept hope alive. "A leader," Napoleon famously said, "is a dealer in hope."

HOPE DIALOGUE
John Gardner, a former senior government official and a brilliant student of leadership, echoes that Napoleonic dictum:
"The first task of a leader is to keep hope alive."
Amen.

Over the long haul, we may well most honor those leaders who are matchless talent developers. But there are indeed times when a "dealer in hope" is essential. Think FDR. Think Churchill. Indeed, think Gerald Ford after the Nixon debacle. In business, think Lee Iacocca at Chrysler in the late 1970s.

6. Leaders Are "Profit Mechanics" (Type III Leadership).

A friend of mine runs a $200 million business. He's as thoughtful as hell, a real people guy. And his presence, if not charismatic, is certainly energetic and reassuring. But that's not the vital secret to his stunning success as CEO over a 15-year period.

My pal majored in mathematics. He loves the *New York Times* Sunday Crossword. And ... more to the point ... he loves the Puzzle-Called-Business.

HIRE HIGHER
There's an old saw in business management: You will be great exactly to the extent that you are willing and eager to hire people who are better than you.

An old, old saw indeed. But no less sharp for being so.

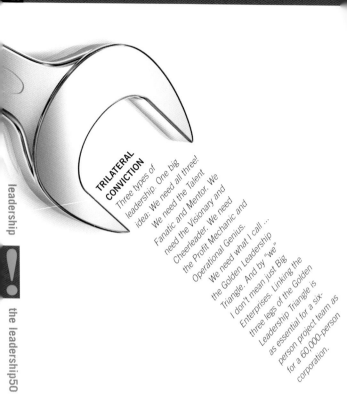

TRILATERAL CONVICTION

Three types of leadership. One big idea: We need all three! We need the Talent Fanatic and Mentor. We need the Visionary and Cheerleader. We need the Profit Mechanic and Operational Genius. We need what I call ... the Golden Leadership Triangle. And by "we" I don't mean just Big Enterprises. Linking the three legs of the Golden Leadership Triangle is as essential for a six-person project team as for a 60,000-person corporation.

The hair stands up on the back of his neck when he examines a P&L or a balance sheet. (Or so I imagine.) He *loves* to tease the most extraordinary conclusions from the biggest, most obscure data sets. It makes him chortle. He hums ... no baloney ... when he plays with numbers. (I've observed it.)

I've come to call this type of leader the IPM: Inspired Profit Mechanic.

An IPM, by himself, would quite possibly be ... a total disaster. On the other hand, the other two leadership types—the Talent Developer and the Visionary—might also end up being disasters unless our friend the IPM is on duty ... humming over those numbers.

7. Leaders Understand That ... It All Depends!

In David McCullough's brilliant biography *John Adams,* one of the author's avowed goals was to resurrect the importance of the dour Adams in the panoply of "Rushmorian candidates who led America at its most precipitous stage of development." Adams is now ascendant. Jefferson is in decline. However, I came away from the book with an entirely different take: First, it led me to do a lot more reading about Jefferson. And second, it led me to believe we were ... damn lucky. We needed ... Adams ... *and* Jefferson ... *and* Washington ... *and* Tom Paine ... *and* Alexander Hamilton ... and James Madison. Remove a single strut from that *and* ... and we're still a colony of Britain. (Perhaps.) Each of those "Rushmorian" individuals had astonishing flaws. Astonishing short-sightedness. As much as they had long-sightedness ... and astonishing strengths.

Message: Leadership is a complex affair! The "Renaissance man (or woman)" is a snare, a myth, a dangerous delusion.

And what's true for the Founding Fathers *(plural!)* is equally true for a start-up restaurant. You need that visionary chef! You need that "people person" who can deal with minimum-wage busboys! You need that IPM who dreams in balance sheets—and who can talk her way around a skeptical banker's objections! In short, you need various strengths at various times.

PROFILE: THE DANCE OF LEADERSHIP

8. Leaders Thrive on Paradox.

Forget what they taught you at the Harvard Business School. The University of Illinois College of Business. The Stanford Business School. The Wharton Business School. Management ain't science! Management is ... 100 percent of the time ... ART.

MANAGEMENT IS AN ... ART. The art of paradox.

leadership

the leadership50

The Ultimate Paradox of Leadership: In order to be "excellent" you must be … CONSISTENT. (By most definitions: Excellence = Consistency of Superior Performance.) But the very moment you begin to excel at "consistency" … you become … TOTALLY VULNERABLE … to attack from the outside.

We must be constantly vigilant about … OPPOSITES.

For example: Are we organized "enough"? If so … WORRY. Are we disorganized "enough"? If so … WORRY.

Worry … constantly … about the balance … the wobble … the swing of the pendulum.

Well, this idea is actually not about … balance. It's about going one way … TOO FAR … for a while … and then going the opposite way … TOO FAR … for a while.

My view: Relatively extreme, wild oscillation between … too much control … and too little control … is probably the secret to long-term effectiveness.

9. Leaders Love the Mess.

Consider these words from the late advertising genius, Jay Chiat: "I'm uncomfortable when I'm comfortable."

Definition of crappy leadership? The leader who needs to be "comfortably" "in control."

Definition of Truly Great Leadership? Leaders who get most energized … when the Shit Hits The Fan.

Leading is … dealing with issues that couldn't be "dealt with" "below you" in the organization. The issues that are laden with ambiguity. A senior exec at AT&T told me, 20 years ago, that if a "problem" arrived in his in-basket that he was capable of deciding on the spot … then something was wrong with the "system." That particular problem should have been solved a level or two

OUT OF ALIGNMENT
The great General Motors CEO Alfred Sloan said that management consisted of … steering back and forth between (a) centralizing-the-hell-out-of-things, which saps creativity, and (b) decentralizing-the-hell-out-of-things, which encourages reckless risk-taking.

My only problem with Sloan's insight: Over the long haul, most organizations net out in the direction of too much centralization. The Control Freaks prevail … and run their organizations into a ditch. (Or off a cliff.)

below him. He earned his hefty paycheck solely by prowling among the intractable issues.

The boss of a 6,000-person systems-engineering company told me that, oddly (his word—"oddly"), the top Project Managers were typically not from the ranks of his highly degreed engineers; instead, they were "the sort who'd been 'AV guys' in high school or college, the ones who are used to facing crisis after crisis after crisis, then grabbing a roll of Duct Tape and fixing The Damn Thing—on the fly and on the spot."

Interesting, eh? One possible message: *Never hire somebody who doesn't bring Duct Tape with him or her to an interview!* (That's certainly how we Vermonters view the matter.) And if not the real thing, at least metaphorical duct tape. Maybe one should plan a crisis in the midst of an interview— a fire alarm or a feigned heart attack. And watch the candidate's reaction. Flustered or calm? Engaged or withdrawn?

The "bottom line" here: In selecting leaders, we must

CHECK YOUR "MESS" KIT
A Penchant for Chaos is particularly necessary in wartime.

During times of peace, a military establishment will tend to promote the "desk jockeys" among the officer corps. But at the proverbial first whiff of grapeshot, you want to find, and invest command in, those who can shine amid the "fog of war,"

as Clausewitz called it.
Enter Grant.
Enter Sherman.
Enter Patton.

be assiduously on the lookout for those who get their jollies in the face of madness ... in the face of chaos that causes others to waffle or fold.

10. Leaders Do!

If you don't know what the hell is going on ... if you don't know the shape of the playing field ... if you don't know the nature of the rule book (or even if there *is* a rule book) ... then, in the immortal words of My Old Man, *"Thomas, don't just stand there. Do something."*

It's a cute phrase. But it's far more profound than that. If you don't know what's going on ... Stop Thinking. (It won't do you much good.) Try ... *something*. See what happens. That is, until you let fly the new system ... or new product ... or new procedure ... or whatever ... you have ... Utterly No Idea What the Hell Is Going On.

11. Leaders Re-Do.

If something goes awry, the typical Big Company ... shoots the messenger ... appoints a Special Investigator ... Aims to make sure that this aberration Never Occurs Again. In the process, the possibility of ... Rapid Progress ... is severely diminished.

In short: "Do it right the first time" is ... stupid. A Snare. A Delusion.

MARIO'S MANTRA
A Need for Speed and a Bias for Chaos go hand in hand. As the great race driver Mario Andretti said, "If things seem under control, you're just not going fast enough." Or: Gentlemen (and ladies), rev your engines!

"FIRE," EVERY TIME
Marketing guru Phil Kotler posits three modern management eras. To paraphrase his view:
1965–1980: The Era of Strategic Planning. The motto of those times: *Ready. Aim. Fire.*
1980–1995: The Era of Global Competitive Warming. The new motto: *Ready. Fire! Aim.*
1995–????: The Era of the Discontinuous Change. The motto of this age: *Fire! Fire! Fire!*

Consider two superstar companies that don't give a second thought to what happens the "first time." (Or the 21st.) Namely: Sony and Microsoft. They "do" ... fast. *And then they ... re-do ... even faster!*

"Sony Electronics," *BusinessWeek* reported, "has a well-earned reputation for persistence. The company's first entry into a new field often isn't very good. But, as it has shown with laptops, Sony will keep trying until it gets it right."

"If Microsoft is good at anything," writes Seth Godin, "it's avoiding the trap [of worrying about criticism]. Microsoft fails constantly. They're eviscerated in public for lousy products. Yet its people persist, through version after version, until they get something that's good enough. And then they can leverage the power that they've gained in other markets to enforce their standard."

The Sony-Microsoft approach is remarkable—and it represents an all too rare trait. Most companies either flog the tepid First Version ... until they look like idiots ... or retreat, deciding that the failure means they weren't supposed to be in the market in the first place.

12. Leaders Know When to Wait.

Yes, leaders act. But (ah, the paradoxes of leadership!) leaders also ... *wait.*

Years ago, I spent an afternoon with Dallas Cowboys President Tex Schramm. He told me he had a third, very special box on his desk ... in addition to an "In" box and an "Out" box.

The extra box: "Too Hard."

The truly troublesome stuff, Schramm told me, he tossed into this third box. Often as not, in a few days or a couple of weeks, something would happen that would provide the key to sorting things out.

Axioms:

1. You need to pick your battles. (Know when to raise and when to fold.)

2. Sometimes inaction promotes sorting out and the preservation of options.

13. Leaders Are Angry.

Jack Welch, the masterful former CEO of GE, is an angry man. So, too, Steve Jobs of Apple Computer. Both imagine Better Universes—and are irritated (mostly at themselves) because those New and Better Universes continue to elude full realization.

Yes, *angry*.

Completely unhinged by the status quo.

Completely and perpetually pissed off by the failure of the sun to rise in the west ... and determined to do something about it.

Right now.

Axiom: Don't ever promote "unangry" people into leadership positions. In fact, don't hire unangry people in the first place.

The ideal job candidate walks in, looks you in the eye, and says, "I can't believe this place is so screwed up. But I'm willing to take a chance—as long as I think I've got a decent shot at changing it." You don't get those types very often. But if you ever do ... hire them on the spot. And pay them whatever the hell they want.

After I published an article on leadership in *Fast Company*, one reader—a senior exec at a financial services firm—offered this idea: "Leaders don't 'want to' win. Effective leaders *need* to win."

Craig Venter, scientist and former CEO of Celera Genomics ... *Needed to Win* ... the race to be the first to map the human genome. Not "desire" (a great starting point) but ... "need." This is a deep psychological issue ... an issue that's certainly somewhere near the epicenter of effective-leadership-in-messy-and-totally-ambiguous-times.

DARK SIDE OF THE MOOD

Is there a Dark Side to this "need"? Of course! All good and useful things are products of excess. And all good things therefore breed their extreme opposite. In this case, the overwhelming "need to win" can produce pathologically anti-social behavior. Hence my emphasis on framing leadership as ... a Dance of Opposites.

Yes, angry.

Completely unhinged by the status quo.

14. Leaders Are Optimists.

Leaders must have not only "fire in the belly" but also
... a smile on their face. Yes, life *is* tough. Some of us
absorb that reality—and then exude the resulting fear and
anxiety through our pores. But effective leaders exude
a sense of confidence and determination that inspires
others. That inspires people to quit licking their wounds
and to ... get on with the (sometimes outrageously
daunting) task at hand.

Reporter Lou Cannon observed the late Ronald
Reagan up-close for many years. His take on what made
the 40th president so effective: Ronald Reagan "radiated
an almost transcendent happiness."

There's also a more elementary way of phrasing this
point: *Leaders show up.* Leaders are there. They keep on
"keeping on." By their very presence, they inspire others
to ... stay the course.

Think Rudy Giuliani, former Mayor of New York
City. Rudy "showed up"—when it really mattered, on
9/11. As one wag put it, he went from being a lame-
duck, philandering husband to being *Time* magazine's
Man of the Year ... in 111 days. How? Not through any
"strategy," well-thought-out or otherwise. But by showing
his face. By standing as the embodiment of Manhattan's
Indomitable Spirit.

Woody Allen said it best:

"Eighty percent of success is showing up."

15. Leaders Convey a Grand Design.

A leader "sets the tone." That's obvious. But a leader is
also ... Chief Architect.

The Chief Architect model: A leader sets out the ...
General Design Parameters. Lets us know what she/he
thinks about quality. About tolerating well-intended and
energetically pursued failures. About innovation. About
logistics performed to perfection.

Call it ... Core Values. Call it ... Essential Philosophy. Call it ... Our Charter. Call it ... Our Constitution. I call it ... THE DESIGN SPECS. The essential ... "stuff" we care about, the way we intend to ... Live and Make Our Mark. The stuff that we won't compromise on. The stuff that is the Essence of our Organizational Character.

Conglomerates (of loosely related enterprises) are out of fashion. For good reason—most have proven unmanageable. But there's one I know that seems to work. That's the Virgin Group. Founder-CEO Richard Branson fits the Chief Architect model to a T. He says he won't launch a new product unless it's "cheeky." (It also has to be of high quality ... and very affordable.)

Branson ... SETS THE DESIGN SPECS. He ... EMBODIES ... LIVES ... THE DESIGN SPECS.

So, too, Welch's Performance Fanaticism and Talent Obsession at GE.

So, too, Lee Iacocca's Pugnaciousness in a Time of Great Darkness at Chrysler.

So, too, Churchill's Determination.

So, too, Gandhi's Persistence.

16. Leaders Attend to Logistical Details.

I love great design! I love scintillating business concepts! But I will be the first—and I hope among the loudest—to acknowledge the basic, day-in-day-out work that lies behind the historically brilliant execution of, say, marketing campaigns at Coca-Cola. Or PepsiCo.

leadership

the leadership50

A MAN OF QUALITY

One of the all-time greats at Conveying a Grand Design— at "setting the tone" and then sending a message— is Roger Milliken, the CEO of Milliken & Co. When Roger undertook his Quality Quest, he developed a fascinating habit. Whenever a factory manager came for a visit, Roger would ride out from corporate headquarters and meet that person at the airport. Knee to knee, they would head back to HQ. And there was one topic of discussion.

Milliken: "What have you done to *dramatically* improve quality in the past 90 days?" And for that factory manager, it was a "good career move" to have a compelling 30-minute spiel at the ready.

Quality was Roger's passion! It wasn't that he knew the answers. To the contrary, he wanted answers that surprised him. But at the level of "Grand Design," he knew precisely the nature of the Quest he wanted all members of the leadership team to be engaged in.

Fact: Much, if not most, of the dot-com implosion of 2000 was a logistics-driven implosion. The sexy stuff—the Web sites and so on—was all in place. But the ability to "deliver the goods," or the toys, at Christmas 1999 was another matter entirely.

For want of a nail, the shoe was lost. For want of a shoe ... (And the next thing you know, you're toast.) Sure, it's an old homily. But it's as true in 2005 as it was hundreds of years ago. Wars—commercial as well as military—are as often won or lost because of an absence of shoes and food and bullets and nails and gasoline ... as they are because of faulty strategy or tactics.

Just ask Gus Pagonis.

Pagonis was the 1991 Gulf War general who got an early battlefield promotion—his third star—from General Norman Schwarzkopf. Why? In astonishingly short order, General Pagonis got the "stuff" to the desert that was needed to support an American force of well over 500,000 people.

Logistics Matter! (Always.)

That was true for George Washington. (Who regularly exited the battlefield at critical moments to travel to Philadelphia, so he could beg the Continental Congress for soldiers' pay and supplies.)

That was true for George Patton. (Whose amazing feats in the Battle of the Bulge would have been even more amazing with a little more fuel for his tanks.)

And that was true for Norman Schwarzkopf and his comrade Gus Pagonis.

"ALL KINDS" BULLETIN

Along about now, I worry that you are ... pulling your hair out.
"Too much. Too much. Too much. How can I do all 50 of these things?" you might say (or scream).

Well, of course you can't do all of these things. But you don't have to. Remember: In leadership, it takes all kinds. Or rather, it takes at least three kinds. (See comments above on the "three leadership types.")

Norman Schwarzkopf didn't need to be Gus Pagonis. He just needed to know that he needed Gus Pagonis. The best leaders recognize and recruit other (different) (extraordinary) leaders.

17. Leaders Side With the "Action Faction."

Bill Creech, the retired four-star general who conducted an extraordinary turnaround at the U.S. Air Force Tactical Air Command, framed the leadership challenge this way: "There's a war on … between the people who are trying to do something and the people who are trying to keep them from doing something wrong."

Creech makes a fascinating point. The "bad guys" ("the people who are trying to keep them from doing something wrong") are rarely representatives of the … Forces of Evil. They are "simply" trying to keep the "action fanatics" from "doing something wrong" … from breaking the rules. In the process, they use "due process" and "compliance" to gum up the works, to slow things down and stifle innovation.

All innovation = Breaking today's rules.

THE COST OF "DOING" IN BUSINESS
Is there a price to be paid for all of this … Rule-Breaking Innovation? Of course!
That price: an Enron here, a Worldcom there.
But: If I were U.S. Secretary of the Treasury, I'd gladly accept the occasional Enron or WorldCom as the necessary price of having a truly entrepreneurial economy.
Likewise: If I were the leader of an eight-person project team, I'd gladly take the heat for the exuberant blunders of a young renegade member … in return for her intense efforts to turn a humdrum project into a … Show-stopper.

In fact, there must always be Total War (right term!) between the Vital Forces of Action and the Necessary Forces of Control.

The problem: The Victors in this Eternal Tug of War … in nine cases out of ten … are the Sanctioned Enforcers of Bureaucratic Rules.

Thus, on balance—and especially in these Traumatically Turbulent Times—one must pursue … IMBALANCE … in favor of the Action Faction.

leadership

the leadership50

PROVOCATION: IF IT AIN'T BROKE, BREAK IT

18. Leaders Honor Rebels.

It's fairly common for companies to pay close attention to their most disgruntled customers. After all, the customers who are roughest on you may potentially lead you to envision and enact critical reforms.

Unfortunately, we rarely extend that idea ("Listen to the dissidents!") to a group that's even more important: *pissed-off* employees.

Recent Gallup research shows that 55 percent of employees are effectively "tuned out." Of the remainder, 19 percent are actively at work sabotaging their company, and 26 percent support their company's current goals and practices.

Conventional wisdom says: Focus on getting more productivity out of the 26 percent. However, I'd contend that the 55 percent typically have damn good reasons for being "tuned out." And the group that interests me most is the 19 percent who are ... active saboteurs. At least they give enough of a damn to do ... *something*.

They are your ... Saviors-in-Waiting. They are the ... Rebels in Your Midst! What if you took their ire ... *seriously?* What if you said it was a ... *fabulous reflection of reality?* What if you ... *listened to them?*

KEEP ON TRUCKIN'

Openness to Upstart Ideas is not something to be ... toyed with. And yet: I love what Michael Dell does in this regard. On his desk, he keeps a plastic bulldozer to remind him not to trample over new ideas.

Hey ... whatever it takes!

---

19. Leaders Hang Out With Freaks.

Innovation is "easy." Spend your time with innovators! Surround yourself with freaks! That's my secret. And I think it'll work for any ... leader.

Message: WE BECOME WHO WE HANG OUT WITH!

Want to become "more interesting"? Hang out with

"more interesting" people. I call it the ... *putting-yourself-in-harm's-way approach.*

BECOME A COLLECTOR!

And here's what you collect: Weird consultants! Weird employees! Weird suppliers! Weird customers! Weird hobbies! Weird vacations! Weird any-damn-thing! As long as it's ... WEIRD.

NEW WEIRD ORDER

A very large corporation once brought me in to introduce its leadership team to "radical" points of view. So I rolled out the old projector and regaled members of the team with a scintillating PowerPoint presentation, right?

No! Instead, I introduced them to ... WEIRD.

They wanted to "get serious about branding." So I introduced them to the best branding freaks I knew: Jean-Marie Dru of TBWA/Chiat/Day. Mickey Drexler of The Gap. Rich Teerlink of Harley-Davidson.

For every opportunity, there is ... Someone Weird.

---

20. Leaders Promote (Weird) Demos.

A leader is determined to start a supply chain revolution. Should he/she bark out an order: "Thou Shalt Overhaul the Supply Chain"?

Maybe. But probably not.

Instead, the leader should make it clear that Supply Chain Overhaul is *the* priority, should make some seed money available, and should ask for quick-and-dirty demos—Demonstration Projects that quickly test, dramatically alter, and greatly improve the idea.

To enhance-cement his/her case, the leader needs:

1. Hard evidence
2. Cool-Weird-Imaginative Evidence
3. A Cadre of Zealous Pioneers (of any rank!)

And he/she needs all this ... Fast.

leadership

!

the leadership50

AN AGING OF "CHANGE"?
A few years ago, when an Irish journalist asked me to state my view of the current state of (corporate) play, I replied: "Twenty years ago we

honored those who didn't 'rock the boat.' Ten years ago we started begging everyone to become a 'change agent.' And, now, in the midst of full-blown madness, I'm asking ...

begging ... 'everyone' to become no less than ... patently disrespectful."

I think he thought I was nuts. But, then, these are nutty times.

"Ordering" the thing done "across the board" usually backfires. That usually results in premature, top-down, staff-run, cookie-cutter approaches—often dominated by the biggest (and thence most conservative) units. But putting out the call for "something, anything, cool, fast" sets in motion a competition, engaging a ... Widespread Band of Sanctioned Pirates ... from anywhere and at any rank in the corporation.

Bottom line: Leaders aiming to change their world ... fast ... identify ... Palpable Heroes ... people in their ranks who have already executed palpable New Look Projects. Then the leaders point to these pioneers and say to the masses: "Look. Here. It looks like this, and it was done by ... one of your own."

DIRECTIONS INCLUDED

For a more complete version of this point ... call it the Director's Cut ... see Chapter 2: "Boss Work: Heroes, Demos, Stories."

---

21. Leaders Make Mistakes.

And they make no bones about it. On the wall of my writing studio in Vermont (along with those photos of FDR and Churchill) hangs a quotation by David Kelley, founder of IDEO Product Design:

"Fail faster. Succeed sooner."

Next to that quote hangs another by the extraordinary photographer Diane Arbus, who told her students:

"Learn not to be careful."

In placid times, leaders may well have ... The Answers. In turbulent times, leaders must have ... The Best Questions. Questions that encourage others to undertake ... Voyages of Mutual Discovery. And the essence of that process: letting people ... *screw up.*

If you try new stuff ... you screw up. If you try ... a lot of new stuff ... you screw up a lot.

Screwing up is the Essence of ... Trying New Stuff.

22. Leaders Make Big Mistakes.

MISTAKES ARE NOT ENOUGH. IN DISCONTINUOUS
TIMES, BIG MISTAKES ARE … MANDATORY.

My all-time favorite PowerPoint slide, among the
thousands in my portfolio: "REWARD EXCELLENT
FAILURES. PUNISH MEDIOCRE SUCCESSES."

These tumultuous times beg for … Bold Initiatives …
to increase the odds … of even staying afloat.

While thoughtless recklessness is not to be
applauded, the word "reckless" must be examined …
carefully. Most who change the world—King, Galileo,
Picasso—were indeed "reckless." But not thoughtless.
They were certainly doing more than "thinking outside
the box." (A tepid term that I loathe!) The Kings and
Galileos and Picassos (and Churchills and de Gaulles) …
attempted … Against Hyper-Long Odds … to Re-imagine
an Entirely New Box. If that ain't "reckless" … I don't
know what the word means.

23. Leaders Create Blame-Free Cultures.

Just making mistakes (even big mistakes) isn't enough.
Creating an error-friendly, blame-free culture is the next—
and all-important—step.

Jorma Ollila has a secret. Ollila is CEO of an
Invention Machine … called Nokia. He transformed a
hodgepodge "conglomerate" into a focused, ferocious
global power. And in *Cold Calling: Business the Nokia*

FAIL, FAIL AGAIN
At first, you **rarely**
succeed.
   Hence, you need to …
fail, fail again.

My summary mantra on
this point goes like this:
   No failures …
no successes.
   No fast failures …

no fast successes.
   No big failures …
no big successes.
   No big, fast failures …
no big, fast successes.

Way, author Trevor Merriden attributes much of Nokia's success to the company's aggressively blame-free, go-ahead-and-try-it corporate culture.

BIG POINT: Honoring "mistakes" and creating a "blame-free" culture does NOT mean ... tolerating sloppy work. Or reneging on accountability.

To the contrary.

The essence of accountability: PEOPLE WHO CARE ... SO DAMN MUCH ... THAT THEY WILL RISK EVERYTHING ... AND SCREW UP BIG-TIME ... IN ORDER TO ACHIEVE THEIR ENDS.

24. Leaders Break Down Barriers.

We are Re-imagining and Re-inventing the World! We are adding value in totally new ways that require ... Bringing to Bear the Entire Resource Set of an Enterprise ... and its Full Supply and Distribution Chain. Which means: No barriers ... whatsoever ... to communication!

NO STOVEPIPES!

("Stovepipe" = an Enclosed Bureaucratic Structure that keeps information in and people out.)

WE HAVE TO LEARN TO TALK TO ONE ANOTHER! SEAMLESSLY! INSTANTLY!

The Demolition of Stovepipes is the Exacting and Detailed ... Work of Top Management. That means: Dirty fingernails. Dive into the details. Do not rest ... until ... ALL THE BULLSHIT ... has been eradicated.

MEASURE YOURSELF: WHAT ... EXACTLY ... HAVE YOU DONE ... TODAY (!) ... IN THE LAST TWO HOURS (!!) ... IN THE LAST MEETING (!!!) ... TO "REMOVE THE BULLSHIT" ... TO "DEMOLISH THE FUNCTIONAL STOVEPIPES" WITHIN YOUR ORGANIZATION?

25. Leaders Forget.

Could it be that the Most Fundamental Job of a Leader is to ... *Forget*?

Edwin Land, the extraordinary inventor and the founder of Polaroid, said that innovation was "not so much having a new idea as stopping having an old idea."

Visa founder Dee Hock made the point equally well: "The problem is never how to get new, innovative thoughts into your mind, but how to get old ones out."

Forgetting!

Bottom line: What if we said that ... THE ESSENCE OF LEADERSHIP IS THE ... WILL TO FORGET?

PEOPLE: A RELATIONSHIP TO TALENT

26. Leaders Are Talent Fanatics.

Yes, I'm aware of the problems of "hype" when it comes to talking about Talent. (I've caused some of those problems.) Nonetheless: "Talent" may be the most potent word I know in the business lexicon.

Use the word ... "Talent" ... and a certain type of image comes to mind. An image that's about as far away from either "employee" or *Dilbert*'s "cubicle slave" as one can imagine.

I think "talent" ... and I conjure up a National League Football team. Or the cast and crew whose production of *The Lion King* I saw in New York a few years ago.

I'm not naïve. And yet I think there's no reason we can't view each and every "employee" as ... TALENT. In fact, I think that's precisely what leaders of the future will ... and must! ... do.

Talent: *Attract it. Nurture it. Mentor it. Reward it. Create the context in which it can thrive.*

So: Are you a ... Certified Talent FANATIC? As the 24-year-old head of a six-person project team? As the 42-year-old head of the public works department for the City of Long Beach? Think about it. Call it the "NFL General Manager Standard." How do you measure up?

"TALENT" FUTURES

The full Talent Treatment ... the complete "why" and "how" of bringing Talent into your orbit, and keeping it there ... comes in Chapter 4: "Boss Job One: The Talent25."

leadership

the leadership50

27. Leaders Nurture Other Leaders.

The honors here go to iconoclast-political-activist-Presidential-candidate Ralph Nader. "I start with the premise," he said, "that the function of leadership is to produce more leaders, not more followers."

The first image that comes to mind when I think about "leadership" is the fabled 1945 picture of Roosevelt, Churchill, and Stalin sitting together on the fantail of the good ship U.S.S. *Quincy*. Hitler is counting his last days. Twenty million Russians are dead. London's been flattened by bombs. And earth's three most potent human beings are quite calmly divvying up the earth, preparing for a post-war environment.

Message: The Leader as ... Strong Man.

But I suspect that those times are past. That the technology is changing ... too fast. As Bill McGowan, co-founder of the telecom upstart MCI, once told me: "The 'chump-to-champ-to-chump' cycle used to be three generations. Now it's about five years."

"Staying power" ... which used to be *mostly* a fantasy ... is now a Total Fantasy. Therefore, I will offer a new guideline for leaders.

Namely: LEADERS DON'T CREATE "FOLLOWERS"! THEY CREATE ENERGIZED, AUTONOMOUS LEADERS. "LEADERS" THROUGHOUT THE ORGANIZATION, STARTING WITH INSPIRED YOUTH AT THE "BOTTOM," HELP OTHERS DISCOVER NEW WORLDS. ENCOURAGE "LEADERS" WHO INVENT NEW WORLDS. LEADERS

leadership

the leadership50

NO STRATEGY, PLEASE—WE'RE MCKINSEY
For 7 years, I worked at McKinsey & Co. The firm has its flaws. (Big flaws.) But for 70-plus years, it's been successful. (Astonishingly successful.)

And one big reason for that success, I contend, is that this renowned strategic consultancy has never had anything approaching a strategy (!).

Meanwhile ... from Day One ... it has been absolutely, persistently obsessed with ... Talent.

As the saying goes: Watch what "they" do, not what "they" say.

WHO OUTSTRIP—AND DETHRONE—THEIR OWN PUTATIVE LEADERS.

I'm not suggesting that everyone is … Einstein. Or Churchill. I *do* mean that everyone *is* responsible for … Making (and Defining) Her/His Own Way. EVERYONE IS CHARGED WITH OVERTURNING TODAY'S BELIEFS.

We can no longer depend on the Big Corporate Fuzzball to nurture us … for 30 or 40 years. Or even 10 or 20 years. Or even … 5 or 10 years. Motto: Everyone a … Renegade. Everyone an … Innovator. Everyone a … Leader.

28. Leaders Engender Trust.

Jim Kouzes, my colleague and the Chairman Emeritus of Tom Peters Company, co-wrote with Barry Posner a book with a fabulous one-word title: *CREDIBILITY*. Jim and Barry insist … based on 20 years of data collection … that at the end of the day … what gives a Leader the ability to … Ask for Great Contributions from people … in a nation or on a seven-person project team … is the degree to which he/she was … Credible.

leadership

the leadership50

"ONE" TRICK PLANNER
Once, after I spoke to the leaders of a financial advisory service company, the CEO said something that has stuck with me. The company's field forces consist entirely of independent contractors, many of whom were then nearing retirement age. The CEO noted that many of these guys would have no one to sell their businesses to. "What they don't understand," he said, "is that the 'trick' to creating a legacy is mentoring. I keep telling them: Spend time developing *just one* person to follow in your footsteps."

I absolutely love that idea: "Just one."

Call it … Credibility.

Call it … Trust.

Superficially, Credibility seems like the "softest" of … Leadership Attributes. And not exactly one that they teach you at Harvard Business School. And yet … over the long haul … Credibility is the Absolute Hardest of Leadership Traits.

I'd not go so far as to say that "Good Leaders" … "never tell a lie." Roosevelt lied like hell as he evaded the Constitution and edged the United States into World War II. To make it through the maze on the way to the top, leaders must exhibit … shrewdness.

And yet … without sounding corny about it … the best of them understand that … Leadership … in the end … is a … Sacred Trust. The responsibilities are enormous. Whether it's Hilda Stewart's Cub Scout Troop, which I belonged to in Severna Park, Maryland, in 1949 … or the one-person counseling sessions between a mentor-professor and her Ph.D. student … or a team of 2,500 at a Fortune 500 giant.

"Trustworthy" is about the biggest—and most sacred—word in the English language.

TRUST OR BUST?

So why don't "they" teach credibility at Harvard Business School? Granted, it's a hard thing to teach. Perhaps my real concern is that the B-school powers-that-be don't seem to give a damn about it. Do they even consider trustworthiness and other "character" issues when they look at prospective students? No, they dwell on Test Scores, blithely ignoring the far-greater long-term importance of a leader's "trust score."

29. Leaders Are Relationship Mavens.

The Age of the Internet notwithstanding, premier sports agent Mark McCormack insists that there are times … and they are by no means infrequent … when one should fly 5,000 miles for a five-minute meeting. I've taken his advice. The wisdom therein is as obvious as the end of your nose. Or at least it should be: LEADERSHIP IS … IN THE END … PURELY PERSONAL … THE ULTIMATE RELATIONSHIP GAME.

When Lou Gerstner took over at IBM, many scoffed (yours truly included) because he lacked a technical background. And yet. Although IBM was touted for providing "great customer service," it had become a bully and had forgotten the ... Art of Intimate Listening. Gerstner hit the road ... visiting customers of all sizes and shapes ... and asking them, point blank, what the hell IBM's problem was. They told him. Point blank. He fixed it. And IBM turned around. Obviously, the story is not that simple, but the impact of Gerstner's Magical Intimate Listening Tour is hard to overestimate.

It's Relationships, Stupid!

30. Leaders Are Networking Fiends.

Some people are ... Instinctive Networkers. Bill Clinton ran around Oxford in the '60s taking detailed notes on damn near everybody he met. I once saw Bob Graham, former Senator from Florida and a 2004 presidential candidate, working a room. WOW! Same deal. Two or three minutes with each person. Sometimes a little less. Rarely more. And as he turned to meet the next person, almost surreptitiously but without fail, he reached into the breast pocket of his suit, pulled out a note card, and jotted something down about the person he had just met.

Even if a large share of "all this" is born rather than made, and training can take us only so far, awareness of ... The Wiring Proclivity ... means paying very explicit

leadership

the leadership50

IT'S RELATIONSHIPS, STUPID!

attention to it in the leadership development process. (Especially in an Age of Instability … where changing arrays of project partners is the New Norm.)

Mantra: LEADERS WEAVE DENSE WEBS OF INCLUSION AT ALL LEVELS. LOSERS ARE SLAVES TO HIERARCHY AND RANK AND FORMAL COMMUNICATION PROCESSES.

> **SIDE RULE**
>
> *My two examples of great networkers are men. But Clinton and Graham are exceptions to their gender. The* rule *is that Women are better at networking than men. Much better.*
>
> *See Chapter 3: "Meet the New Boss: Women Rule."*

31. Leaders Connect.

Great Leaders really are … THERE. They really are … INTENSELY CONCENTRATED ON YOU. They really are … REAL. They … CONNECT.

There's nothing I'd rather do than meet the most extraordinary human being alive today: Nelson Mandela. And I know without a trace of doubt that if I met him, I'd come away from the 2.5-minute meeting with the impression that Mandela had thought I was … THE MOST INTERESTING PERSON ON EARTH.

That is exactly what … Great Leaders … "do."

There's an intriguing story that goes more or less like

this: Ms. X had sat at dinner between Mr. Y and Mr. Z. Mssrs. Y and Z were renowned individuals. Z in particular. Said Ms. X about Mr. Y, "When you sat at dinner with him, you came away believing that he was perhaps the smartest individual you'd ever met." About Mr. Z (the *truly* successful one), she said, "When you sat at dinner with Mr. Z, you came away

Leaders weave dense webs of inclusion at all levels.

thinking that *you* were the smartest person on earth."
I've been somewhat misleading in making this point,
and a few others. I imply that there are some tried and
true "techniques" ... that will allow you to master the
"relationship thing." I do believe we can get better at
the "relationship thing." (I have a no-nonsense friend I
bludgeoned into doing thank-you notes; he calls it "life-
transforming.") But I think, in the end, unless you are
a "relationship sort"—and I'm not sure how much of
this can be learned or taught—you're going to have the
devil's own time with these ideas. Because Investing
in Relationships means two big things: (1) SINCERITY.
(2) TIME. Neither can be faked. Frankly, if you don't
truly enjoy people ... there's not much hope in terms of
Leadership Effectiveness. For those who are choosing
leaders ... beware.

PROFESSION: THE "JOB" OF LEADING

32. Leaders Push Their Organizations.

In particular, they push their organizations to move up,
up, up the Value-Added Ladder. Making "good stuff" is
no longer enough. Not by a long shot. "Good stuff" has
become but the ... Starting Point. In fact, even "Great
Stuff" has assumed near-commodity status.

"These days," said Ann Livermore, head of Hewlett-
Packard's services division, "building the best server isn't
enough. That's the price of entry." That remark was made
on the heels of an *$18 billion* offer that Hewlett-Packard
made in 2000 for PricewaterhouseCoopers, with its
31,000 consultants.

The idea: Services Added. And Intellectual Capital
Added. And lots of both!

Question: What about *your* flavor of "turnkey-
services-added"? (You'd best have a ... Brilliant and All-
Encompassing ... answer.)

33. Leaders Create New Markets.

I posit a simple rule: NO ONE EVER MADE IT INTO THE ... BUSINESS HALL OF FAME ... ON A RECORD OF LINE EXTENSIONS.

Think Gates. (Microsoft.) McNealy. (Sun.) Ellison. (Oracle.) Dell. (Dell.) Jobs. (Apple.) Bezos. (Amazon.) Welch. (GE) Walton. (Wal*Mart.) Blank & Marcus. (Home Depot.) Carnegie. Rockefeller. Sloan. Ford.

Does "line extension" come to mind?

Hardly.

The short list above is not marked by champions of look-alikes. Some (Jobs, Ellison, McNealy) were brilliant Product Innovators. Some (Dell, Gates, Bezos, Welch, Sloan) were brilliant Business Systems Innovators. But all were ... Market Creators.

There's another (huge) problem with the "line extension" mentality at Huge Co. Most Huge Co. "hurdle rates" demand ... Big Bucks ... fast ... from those "line extensions." What's wrong with that? Plenty, it turns out.

Fact: Most re-defining products start out as little niche ideas that take off ... and change the world ... only years later.

34. Leaders Love New Technology.

Technology ... *is* ... changing ... *everything*. I'm not insisting that every leader must also be a Chief Technology Officer. That's too much to ask, especially from the 52-year-old Big Boss of Enormous Corp.

But I am insisting on something *specific*. Something *verifiable*. Something *BIG*. Name: That 52-year-old CEO need not be able to hack Enormous Corp.'s computer network. But she does need to be ... DESPERATELY ...

leadership

the leadership50

HOPELESSLY ... IN LOVE ... WITH NEW TECHNOLOGY.

I'm hardly a young, dewy-eyed technologist. To be (far too) honest, the last programming language I learned was ... FORTRAN. My kids "get" the Web far better than I do. (Understatement.) But I am a ... PASSIONATE APPRECIATOR of technology.

My strong belief: Effective Leaders ... must ... DEEPLY APPRECIATE (in the fullest sense of that word, meaning both "understand" and "value") ... the New Technologies ... and instinctively "get" their power to topple all regnant industry wisdom.

35. Leaders Are Salespeople Extraordinaire.

Leaders know that it's ... ALL SALES, ALL THE TIME.

Leadership = Sales.

PERIOD.

Don't agree? Don't ask me.

Ask George W. Bush. Ask William J. Clinton. And ask ... the successful "chief" of a six-person project team who was able to induce Significant Change in the way her 600-person division handles logistics.

Doubtless she had a good idea.

Doubtless she has good technical skills. Beyond doubtless:

She is ... a Great Salesperson.

Axiom: If you don't LOVE SALES ... find another life. And don't pretend to be a "leader."

(Harsh ... but true.)

ALL SALES, ALL THE TIME

36. Leaders Love "Politics."

POLITICS. I've observed that most "staffers" hate it. They consider it ... "slimy" ... "demeaning" ... "wasteful."

They're wrong.

They're stupid. (Sorry.)

LOVE POLITICS ... OR DON'T EXPECT TO GET ANYTHING DONE DURING YOUR TENURE.

Politics = Getting Things Done Through People.

leadership = sales. PERIOD.

Compromising. (True!)

Listening. (All the time!)

Standing your ground ... upon occasion. (Even if it costs you dearly to do so.)

Giving in ... upon occasion. (Again, even if it costs you dearly to do so.)

There's nothing that gets my goat more than the "scientist" or "engineer" or "administrator" who says to me, "It's all just damned politics. I don't have the stomach for it."

People who govern in times of war ... *do politics*.

People who get scientific papers accepted at prestigious journals ... *do politics*.

People who win Nobel Prizes ... *do politics*.

People who manage immense undertakings like the Human Genome Project ... *do politics*.

People who lead the effort to get a community center built ... *do politics*.

Sure, politics is sometimes downright dirty. Yet ... politics ... is all about human beings succeeding (or failing) at achieving something by working together. That's true in government ... in marriage ... or in a business setting.

So: IF YOU DON'T LOVE POLITICS ... YOU'LL NEVER GET ANYTHING DONE. YOU ARE NOT A LEADER.

NIX POPULI

Politics rules! You must learn to maneuver smoothly around the rough edges of human behavior and institutional dynamics.

But: All significant change occurs in direct confrontation with forces of "the establishment." (That's why they call it "change"!)

Thus: All significant change is ... war. War on "the way we've always done things around here." So if you believe you can "do change" without breaking a little china (or a lot of it), I suggest that you... GET A LIFE.

Message: If you're desperately pursuing victory in a popularity contest, then you are not a leader.

37. Leaders Master Their Organizations.

Jill Ker Conway was the first woman president of
Smith College. She confronted a (very) recalcitrant and
entrenched bureaucracy. Her quandary: Fight 'em?
Or go around 'em?

Ms. Conway was in a hurry! She had no time for
protracted fights. So her answer was (obvious-in-
retrospect): SURROUND THE BASTARDS!

Ms. Conway's strategy, I believe, has universal
applicability:

1. Effective Leaders Are Masters of the End Run.

2. Effective leaders mostly avoid—rather than fight—
the "Old Culture." (Be polite. But don't expend most of
your precious hours trying to change 'em.) (At least until
you've "won"—in which instance they will be among
the first to rush aboard and tell you how they've always
secretly supported you.)

3. Effective leaders know that while you can't
change "people," you can change "cultures"—by finding
and promoting people and projects ... that effectively
demonstrate "The New Way."

4. Effective leaders "follow the money." They find ...
new funding sources ... to launch the novel programs that
will define your tenure.

NOW AND ZEN

*Check out the section called "Zen and the Art of Culture Change"
in Chapter 2: "Boss Work: Heroes, Demos, Stories" for an extended
discussion of Jill Ker Conway's masterly strategy.*

---

38. Leaders Are Great Learners.

The best (and brightest) consultant I worked with in my
seven years at McKinsey had, I thought, one True Secret:
He fearlessly and invariably asked, "WHY?"

"WHY?" is ... sooooo ... powerful! It is Tool Number
One of every Intrepid Explorer! And not nearly so
innocent as it sounds.

It's damn tough for a Leader ... who some contend
is supposed to "know the answers" ... to humbly and

repeatedly ask ... regarding the "simplest" issues ... WHY? And yet, in those so-called "simple" situations, it is the unasked "Why?" that's usually the key to the mint.

For years (and years ...), nobody asks, "Why?" about this or that procedure. ("Hey ... it's the way we do things around here.")

Hence: Effective Leading = Invariably Asking "WHY?"

At least a dozen times a day.

So ... repeat after me:

why?

why?

why?

39. Leaders Are Great Performers.

FDR claimed, "It is necessary for the President to be the nation's No.1 actor."

Is this a plug for disingenuous behavior?

No. (Or mostly not.)

If a leader attempts to induce risk taking ... then she or he must *embody* risk taking, even if she or he is a naturally reticent person.

As one of my friends put it, bluntly, "Look, Tom, leaders aren't allowed to have bad days, especially on bad days. From the retail battlefield to the real thing, leaders must exude the energy and confidence that will embolden others to act in the face of peril. It's that simple. And that hard."

Every move by a leader—a 24-year-old supervisor, or the President of the United States—is scrutinized and dissected with respect to what it portends for the organization (and for every individual in it).

Hence: Act ... accordingly!

40. Leaders Are Great Storytellers.

A scintillating *story* makes an (abstract) strategy real. Brings it to life. Ronald Reagan had a handful of beliefs that were truly dear to him. And he held onto them ... despite the insane pressures of the presidency. Above all, Ronald Reagan was ... a Great Storyteller. (You can love him or hate him. But you can't deny his splendid storytelling ability, or the degree to which it changed the overall dialogue in America—for the better!)

It's simple. It's profound. It's something that most scientists, engineers, and their ilk are simply incapable of getting. (I'm only half kidding.)

So: What's your (compelling) story?

> **THE "LEAD" STORY**
> *Howard Gardner: "A key—perhaps the key—to leadership is the effective*
> *communication of a story." More (much more) on this point in*
> *Chapter 4: "Boss Work: Heroes, Demos, Stories."*

leadership

the leadership50

PASSION: THE "INSIDE" GAME

41. Leaders Enjoy Leading.

At the end of a seminar in Dublin a few years ago, the head of a marketing services company approached me, made some very complimentary remarks about my commentary on leadership ... and proceeded to say that I'd missed the most important point. "Leaders," he insisted, "must get a kick out of leading."

He has a (brilliant) point.

So ... with thanks ... here it is.

An historian claimed that Franklin Roosevelt, crippled though he was, couldn't wait to get to his desk in the morning—he loved being President so much. On the other hand, Warren Bennis, the leadership guru and my great friend, did a stint as president of the University of Cincinnati, and was often unhappy in that role. He said an old friend spotted the source of his problem with frightening acuity: "Warren," the friend said, "you want to *'be'* president, but do you want to *'do'* president?"

Leading isn't for everyone! Take me, for example. I love what I do—the researching and writing and presenting bits. But I do not get an "unmitigated kick," as one of my leader pals put it, out of the issues that occupy the day of a true leader. And that's that. I award myself a few points for having had the good sense to recognize this—and thus, within my own company, I "delegate" the CEO job to someone else, who does get her kicks out of coming to the office in the morning and finding a host of intractable "people problems" awaiting.

Message: If you don't *love* leading, look ... quickly ... for the nearest exit. Do *not* try to fake it.

42. Leaders Know Themselves.

Leadership is ... personal.

Leaders must first and foremost: *Know Themselves. Be aware of their impact on others. Have an Honest Coach who can Shoot Straight with them.*

LEADERS—AT ANY LEVEL!—HAVE AN ENORMOUS RESPONSIBILITY. (They are responsible for the Development and Future of Others!)

The frightening fact is that leaders ... do make a (potentially huge) difference.

For good.

Or for ill.

And they make that difference as a result of ... the way they present themselves.

Inspired Leadership (in a Telemarketing Center, or

Leaders must first and foremost:
Know themselves.

in mentoring a single Ph.D. student) is a ... MUTUAL DISCOVERY PROCESS. And you cannot engage in a "liberating mutual discovery process" unless you are comfortable with yourself.

MUTUAL DISCOVERY ... means (by definition) confronting the unknown head-on, fearlessly taking the ambiguous path. "Leaders" who are not comfortable with themselves tend to be control freaks. They need to constantly remind you of Who's in charge. ("I am!") Of course, what they are really doing is trying to convince *themselves* that they are in charge!

KNOW THY IGNORANCE

Recall that marvelous phrase offered by Karl Weick: "I DON'T KNOW." Three short words, one HUGE principle. The Bald Fact is that "I DON'T KNOW" is an act of the Utmost Bravery ... on the part of the Leader. It suggests a willingness to ... Cede Control.

Maybe leadership is the opposite of what it seems: LEADING IS GRANTING "EXPLORATION RIGHTS" TO ONE'S "FOLLOWERS." Remember that the idea of "followership" is really about ... Creating More Leaders.

I think all of this makes sense. Common sense. (Or maybe, alas, *un*common sense.) If "excellence," for example, is the goal, especially amid today's madness, then leaders ... must have ... the Full Emotional Engagement ... of their "followers"/"explorers."

Corollary point: People are only 100 percent engaged if they perceive themselves to be in complete charge of their Personal Quests.

And again, you-the-leader will only permit that level of growth, and thence experimentation and subsequent failure, if you are secure with ... YOU. That is, if you get an Unmitigated Kick Out of the Mess.

GOOD HUMOR MANAGER
Leaders who are at peace with themselves also laugh a lot. Thus, here are two of my rules:

1. Never work in a place where laughter is rare.
2. Never work for a leader who doesn't laugh.

43. Leaders Accept Responsibility.

It's simple: *Leaders take responsibility—visibly!—for the decisions they make and for the outcomes that ensue.* At any level, at any age, in any position of responsibility. To play the "Blame Game" destroys the ... CREDIBILITY ... of a "leader" faster than any other single act.

> **LEGAL WEASELS**
> *Leaders do not "take the Fifth" on national television, as senior officers from giant companies like Enron and WorldCom were seen doing in 2002. Yes, that was their right. Yes, that was the legally smart thing to do. But leadership and legalism don't mix.*

But there's even more to it than that: By avoiding any semblance of scapegoating, leaders make it clear that the Blame Game simply ain't "on"—and is *(per se)* cause for dismissal or at least severe reprimand.

Does this mean that retrospective analysis of things that go awry is inappropriate? Of course not. Yes, I've argued for 20 years that "a bias for action" is the single most significant positive attribute a successful enterprise can have. Yet a "bias for action" does *not* entail thoughtlessness about the past. However, it does suggest that there is a limit to the amount of introspection that companies should indulge in. The best response to a screw-up is to do a dab of retrospective assessment—and then, hastily, get on with the next project.

Simple fact: Huge bureaucracies think too much ... and act too little. "Scapegoating" is a big part of that debilitating, paralytic process.

44. Leaders Focus.

The very creative leader of an educational foundation, a friend of mine, was about to embark on a program to expand his extraordinary school to a nationwide system of schools that embody his philosophy. He was at one of those "inflection points" ... where the emphasis shifts from "making one great institution" to "making a great *system* of institutions." His foundation has an advisory board, and the chairman of that board—the former

leadership

the leadership50

chairman of CVS/pharmacy—offered this insight: "Your number-one priority is creating a 'To-Don't' list."

Fantastic! A "TO-DON'T" LIST!

Our sage advisor went on to advise my insanely talented colleague to sit down once a week, or at least once a month, with a friendly-but-formal "To-Don't Advisor" to review his calendar ... and consider what might have been eliminated during the last few days or weeks, and what ought to be eliminated during the coming days and weeks.

Nice:

1. Formal "To-Don't" list.

2. Formal "system" to "manage" the "To-Don't" list.

Fact: There's nothing ... NOTHING! ... easier than writing a 50-item "TO-DO" list. In which ... EACH ONE OF THE 50 ITEMS is ... truly of the Utmost Importance.

Fact: During a six-year tour as Finance Chief or Housekeeping Chief (or whatever)... GETTING ONE COOL THING DONE ... IS A V-E-R-Y BIG DEAL. And a damn-difficult deal—if you don't learn to focus.

45. Leaders Take Breaks.

The demands of leadership at any level could fill one's waking hours thrice over, especially these days. And at times, 18-hour days are a must. But ... beware of burnout. Be more aware of being *unaware* of burnout.

This is not a homily about "work-life balance." This is a warning: Stress may kill. Literally. And it surely kills personal and organizational effectiveness!

Antidote? That's up to you. A few deep-breathing breaks, or two-minute-eyes-closed meditative stints, can be invaluable during the course of the day. So, too, a

ORDER OF BATTLE
When James Schlesinger was preparing to become U.S. Secretary of Defense back in the 1970s, he got some shrewd advice from Col. Richard Hallock: "You must understand that if you want to leave a legacy it is vital for you to make a quick decision about what you want that legacy to be ... because after several months you become so caught up in the business of the Pentagon ... that it will be too late. Pick a few projects and put the full weight of your office behind them. Guide the projects. Nurture them. Know from the very beginning that they will be your legacy."

TO-
DON'T
LIST

1.
2.
3.
4.
5.
6.
7.
8.
9.
10.

long holiday—and the occasional four-day weekend. Such breaks are essential, and you probably need some active coaching-intervention to pull it off.

One more thing: The tougher the circumstances, when breaks are "impossible," the more you need a break! For FDR, taking a break took the form of spending regular time with his stamp collection. Makes sense to me.

Message I: Zombies are rotten leaders!

Message II: Zombies are the very last to realize that they are ... Zombies!

46. Leaders Are the Brand.

Brand is a "character issue." Hence "branding" is ... personal. A Pure Leadership Issue. The leader—Welch at GE, Goizueta at Coca-Cola, Gates at Microsoft, Jobs at Apple, Branson at Virgin Group—*is* the brand.

While a slew of programs may support a brand, it is the moment-to-moment actions of Nike's Phil Knight or Oracle's Larry Ellison that define the brand.

Essential fact: There is no "minutiae" for leaders. Whether you are that 24-year-old, fresh-caught Project Team Leader ... or Top of the Totem Pole ... all of the people who work for you are Inveterate Readers of Tea Leaves. *Your* Tea Leaves.

That is, they are looking (for instance) at the way you spend your time. The way you spend your time ... in detail ... Illustrates Exactly What You Care About.

Manage yourself! Watch yourself!

You will live or die ... as Leader ... by the degree to

BREATHING 101: WHAT I DID LAST SUMMER

On the surface, my life is a lark. But it felt like no lark as I headed into the summer of 2004. The work had suddenly ceased to be either fun or rewarding.

So on 7 June 2004, I traveled to Canyon Ranch/Berkshires for a five-week stint. Report: Unequivocally the best five weeks in my life.

Yoga. Chi Gong. Tai Chi. West African drumming. Visualization. Mind-mapping. Massage. Pilates. Sound therapy.

And ... *learning to breathe!*

It took me five weeks. At age 61, odd as it sounds, I began to learn to breathe ... and it saved my life and is helping to save (or at least helping me find) my soul.

As to my work, I was re-energized, as I hadn't been in a decade. I got wildly excited about getting back on the road, and beginning to put much deeper meaning into what I do.

which … Your Calendar … Reflects Your Brand Priorities.
Summary:

1. You = Your Calendar.
2. You = The Brand.
3. Ergo … The Brand = Your Calendar.

47. Leaders Express Their Passion.

In their book *The Leader's Voice,* my colleagues Boyd
Clarke and Ron Crossland argue as follows: "Vision is a
love affair with an idea." Nice.

"Vision" is not something created by a … committee.

"Vision" is not something generated by … analysis.

"Vision" is not something cooked up by a …
management consultant.

"Vision" is about … wild, intemperate … LOVE.

When I started writing about leadership, I created a
PowerPoint slide that surprised me. I said leadership was
… "all about love."

"Love" as I define it: *Passion. Appetite for life.
Engagement. Commitment. Great causes and the
determination to make a difference. Shared adventures.
Bizarre failures. Growth. Insatiable appetite for change.*

POSTSCRIPT: TOWARD A LEGACY

48. Leaders Know When to Leave.

There's a time to come. And … a time to go.

People who are great at "roiling the waters and stirring up change" are, typically, woefully inept at "keeping the damn thing afloat" once it's been launched within "the system."

None of us, it turns out, are "men (or women!) for all seasons." We are men and women for a *particular* season. That is, we are at our best for a short period of time.

Think about it.

49. Leaders Do Stuff That Matters.

Sometimes I think that all "leadership literature" stinks— and that includes my stuff, too. Too much of it focuses on tactics and motivation (and, frankly, manipulation). And it misses the point: *Leadership for what?*

From King and Gandhi and Jefferson … to Bill Gates and Steve Jobs and Richard Branson … leaders lead because they want to get Some Particular Thing … *Done*. They want to … Do Stuff That Matters.

Steve Jobs aimed to change the world … with an "Insanely Great" (his term) idea about what a computer could be. Staying with the tech industry, you could say the same about Michael Dell. So, too, Larry Ellison at Oracle. Or, in the world of financial services, you could point to Ned Johnson at Fidelity. Or to Charles Schwab.

Those and other Great Leaders are not (merely) great at "leading." They are great at inducing others to take novel journeys to … Places of Surpassing Importance.

PIRATE PROJECT
I took a real shine to Tracy Kidder's 1981 book *The Soul of a New Machine*, the saga of building a very risky—and eventually very successful—mini-computer at Data General.

I particularly recall the process that project leaders went through to "sign up" team members. ("Sign-up"—their term.)

Remember, back in those days (the late '70s), taking risks was unusual.

But DG's pirate-leaders asked the best-and-the-brightest to eschew the mainstream company project and "sign up" … to join them in a low-odds adventure to … Change the World.

"Vision is about…
wild, intemperate… LOVE."

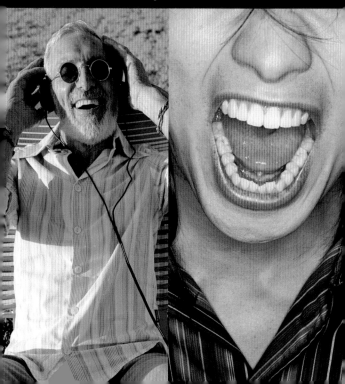

50. Leaders ...

In an earlier (and much different) version of this list that I wrote for *Fast Company* magazine, I asked readers to submit their definitions of "leadership." Of the 287 replies I received, many were at least as "on point" as my own preliminary observations. Here are my favorites:

"Hire smart. Go bonkers. Have grace. Make mistakes. Love technology. Start all over again."

"Leadership is the process of engaging people in Creating a Legacy of Excellence."

"Leaders are living individuals whose presence employees can smell, feel, touch."

"Leaders sweat the small stuff, the 'cultural give-aways,' like clean employee parking lots."

"'It's only business, not personal': IT IS ALWAYS PERSONAL."

"Leaders love their work. That passion is infectious."

"Leaders have a kid alive in them."

"Leaders ooze integrity."

"Leaders are never afraid to walk away from [bad] business."

"Leaders communicate relentlessly."

"Leaders select their battles carefully."

"Real leaders don't always get their way."

"Leaders care."

"Leaders serve."

And my absolute favorite:

"Leaders Need to be the Rock of Gibraltar on Rollerblades."

TOP 10 TO-DOs

1. *Say* ... Make "I don't know" a central, strategic part of your leadership lexicon. Uncertainty is here to stay. Acknowledging it is a Show of Strength.

2. *See* ... Keep your inner eye on the Grand Possibilities that lie beyond—nay: *within*—the uncertainty all around you. Be (per Napoleon) a "dealer in hope."

3. *Do* ... Become an Action Figure. Life is too short—business life is too chaotic—to "get it right" first. When in doubt (especially when in doubt!) ... DO SOMETHING!

4. *Fail* ... Accept mistakes as the price of Greatness. Post a sign in your office that says "REWARD EXCELLENT FAILURES. PUNISH MEDIOCRE SUCCESSES"— and keep it always in view.

5. *Weave* ... Remember that bringing people together—not ordering them about— is Job One for all leaders in our Disruptive Age.

6. *Plan* ... Tend to your Legacy by making *specific* arrangements for people to succeed you. Mantra: Mentor, mentor, mentor!

7. *Act* ... Cultivate the Art of Leadership— in particular, the Art of Performance. Leading well is a Confidence Game of the Highest Sort. So ... Act the Part.

8. *Prune* ... Clear away the mass of clutter that undermines your Sense of Focus. Create a To-Don't list, add stuff to it regularly, and "follow" it religiously.

9. *Chill* ... Know when to take a break. When colleagues ever-so-carefully warn you against burnout, listen to them. Schedule regular vacations (long ones—not a three-day weekend here or there), and keep to that schedule.

10. *Love* ... Laugh, smile, and (in every way possible) express your Passion for What You Do.

COOL FRIEND: Steve Farber

Steve Farber was a colleague of mine at the Tom Peters Company, where he was "Vice President and Official Mouthpiece" (that's what it said on his business card). Today, he is president of Extreme Leadership, Inc., a leadership consulting company. Below are some remarks he made on the occasion of publishing his recent book, **The Radical Leap: A Personal Lesson in Extreme Leadership** *(2004).*

* *

Ultimately the motivator of a leader is love. It comes down to the heart. It's love of something or someone. Love of the cause, of the principle, of the idea, of the future that you're trying to create, love of the people that you're serving and the people that you're working with. That's really where the energy comes from.

* *

On the subject of love, one of the characters in the book … says the ideal is, "Do what you love in the service of people who love what you do." That covers everything as far as I'm concerned.

* *

The first part, "do what you love," is your own connection to your work. That's where you get your energy. How can you expect your customers to love doing business with you if you don't love your business yourself? People have a pretty sophisticated bullshit meter and they know when you're faking it. I'm not talking about the metaphysical "do what you love and the money will follow" hoo-ha stuff. If you're in love with your work you're going to bring more energy and imagination and creativity to it. And you're going to have the juice to work through the obstacles. But it's not doing what you love just *because.* The ethical context or moral context, or whatever you want to call it, is "in the service of people."

* *

Leaders should see themselves as being in the service of the people that they're leading. You're creating the best possible environment for them to do the best possible work. And it's also in the service of the people that you're selling to, essentially, and those people should "love what you do." That doesn't mean go out and only do business with the people who already love you. It should be at the core of everything that you're trying to create.

* *

I use the phrase "extreme leadership" to try to move people off the mark a little bit and get them thinking that leadership is not about your position, it's not about your title, and you're not a leader just because your org chart says you are. Having said that, the higher up you go in an organization, the greater the expectation is that you'll lead and not just manage.

* *

When you walk into the reception area of a company you've never visited before, you can tell within 30 seconds whether or not the place is exciting and cool, whether they're doing interesting work, or whether it's a morgue.

As an Extreme Leader, it's your job to generate energy in the environment and in the people around you.

There are people that get very energetic about—from the outside looking in—seemingly mundane things. There was a great article in the *Wall Street Journal* a number of years ago about how Gillette has managed to create an environment that's entirely energetic about razor blades. They are completely stoked about ... shaving!

To hear people talk about the product of developing great shaving technology and how they get so excited about it is really inspiring.

* *

"Extreme leadership" is a redundant phrase, because if somebody's really leading, what they're doing is already extreme. Leadership is the act of transformation. Taking nothing and turning it into something.

2

BOSS WORK: HEROES, DEMOS, STORIES

Contrasts

Was	Is
Top-down leadership	Tap-the-grassroots
Planning, planning	Projects, projects
Issuing orders	Finding heroes
Micro-managing	Dramatizing demos
Telling people what to do	Telling stories
Promotion by seniority	Promotion as "story"
"Running the show"	Building a portfolio
Working "through channels"	Walking through barriers
Dilbert-ville	WOW-land
Resigned to "life"	Ready to Change the World

!Rant

We are not prepared ...

We still think in terms of *planning* and *ordering* change. • We speak of "systematic implementation throughout the enterprise." But there's no longer time for that. • We must, instead, view leadership as a matter of **FOSTERING AND THEN ENDORSING COOL AND BOLD EXPERIMENTS** ... aka WOW Projects ... that arise from deep within an organization. • We must understand that every boss's top job is not to "make change" but to *find* and *celebrate* **change makers**—hidden heroes who contribute to a **SCINTILLATING PORTFOLIO OF WOW PROJECTS**, and whose work inspires others-by-the-bushel to step out from hiding and mimic them.

!Vision

I imagine ...

A 123-person IT Department. The department head, Ava Jamison, has five senior project managers who report to her, and **she treats each of them as a venture capitalist** who deals with a "portfolio"— **A PORTFOLIO OF WOW PEOPLE AND WOW PROJECTS.** • Ava (a VC herself!) regularly asks each of her VCs to report on how their portfolio is "performing," and they respond with **GRIPPING STORIES** about **REVELATORY DEMOS** conducted by **FRONT-LINE HEROES**.

 • Did Ava "order" all this to happen? Hardly. She framed a few **inspiring guidelines for the direction of the department.** ("Awesome Customer Experiences." **"LIGHTNING-FAST INNOVATION."** Whatever.) And she charged her VCs to let a thousand WOW stories bloom. • But when it comes to creating a Cool New Culture, Ava is merely "fertilizing" a **GORGEOUS GARDEN OF WOW** that is growing like Topsy all around her. Now, *that's* Boss Work!

Out of Order: How Not to "Boss"

Being "the boss" isn't what it used to be. Mostly, that's a Very Good Thing. And a surprisingly easy thing. But it can be incredibly hard to give up the old habits of Management by Exhortation and Management by Detailed Plan. Consider the persistent tendency among managers to issue orders *ex cathedra*—orders like the following:

"Get more entrepreneurial."

"Take risks."

"Implement a zero defects program."

"Empower people."

STUPID.

STUPID.

STUPID.

Why? *Regardless of your official rank, "ordering" systematic change is ... a waste of time.* Trying to "order a new culture" into being doesn't work. Maybe it worked once upon a time. (Though I doubt even that.) But the boss who operates that way today will find himself going nowhere fast. And maybe even backwards. Those "clear" orders will be "executed" by Frustrated Middle Managers bent on preserving their rapidly disintegrating power base— they will become the worst sort of Innovation Quashers.

The goal of "boss work" must be this: Get people initiating, and then working on, what I call WOW Projects! Projects that they put their heart and soul into! Projects that they will want to be remembered by! (Ask yourself: Do you want people working for you who *don't* want to be remembered by what they're doing ... right now?)

To take the idea a step further: You, the boss, must turn your company into a place where ... Amazing Stuff ... is *always* percolating. Task One is gathering an awesome array of Incredibly Cool People, people who invest in, and commit to, and execute, an awesome array of Bold Experiments. Bold Experiments that turn into ... that Awesome Array of WOW Projects.

> **WOW: THE WORD**
>
> *What do I mean by "WOW Project"? The following is by way of a definition. (See also* Essentials: Talent *for more on this key topic.)*
>
> *Project: a task that has a beginning and an end, as well as deliverables along the way.*
>
> *WOW Project: one that has "goals and objectives" that inspire … and inspire others.*
>
> *WOW Projects are …*
>
> *Projects that Matter.*
> *Projects that Make a Difference.*
> *Projects that you can Brag About … forever.*
> *Projects that Transform the Enterprise.*
> *Projects that Take Your Breath Away.*
> *Projects that make you/me/us/"them" Smile.*
> *Projects that Highlight Why … You Are Here on Earth.*
> *WOW Projects are … not hype.*
> *WOW Projects are … a necessity.*

Boss Work That Works

"I'm trying to 'lead change' and induce 'risk-taking' at my company. Got any ideas?"

If I've been asked that question once, I've been asked it a hundred times. In fact, after 25 years on the seminar circuit, I've probably heard it a thousand times. The questioner is usually a mid-level boss, running a middle-sized department in a middle-sized division of some not-so-middle-sized company.

She says, "I have a pretty good idea of where we need to go. And I can vaguely sketch the outlines of the new 'culture' that I think we need. I trust my instincts, even though I don't have all the details ironed out. But I'm having trouble getting people to line up behind me. So …

"Got any ideas?"

For years, in response to this question, I waffled. I'd launch a little rant on leadership. Or I'd give a nod to empowerment. Whatever. Not wrong. But not right, either.

BOSS WRECK
Perhaps master-guru Peter Drucker should be declared this chapter's official muse. He once wrote: "So much of what we call management consists in making it difficult for people to work."
Hence this New Boss Job Description: GET THE HELL OUT OF THE WAY AND LET THOSE WITH THE COOLEST IDEAS BATTLE FOR SUPREMACY.

Lately, I've changed my tune.

"There is only One Way," I boldly proclaim.

"Find Heroes. Do Demos. Tell Stories."

To elaborate:

We need *heroes: Mortal Exemplars* of the Exciting New Way of Doing Things.

We need *demos: Palpable Proof* that this Exciting New Way of Doing Things is eminently do-able.

We need *stories: Riveting Tales* that fire the imagination of ... as-yet-reluctant heroes-in-waiting.

The "Lead Frog" Strategy

I recently happened upon a phrase that perfectly encapsulates my argument about Boss Work: If you want to "leapfrog" change ... well, then, you need *"Lead Frogs."*

Hence, the "Lead Frog" strategy.

It goes like this: Troll through the ranks for would-be revolutionaries—people who have long been itching to make things happen. (Or who are already harboring success stories that they're afraid to go public with ... for fear of the Old Guard's wrath.) Given half a chance, these extant or prospective Lead Frogs will leap over the Fortress of Inertia ... and mark out a visible path that others can follow.

The obvious corollary: Don't waste precious time (at least not yet) on the Reluctant Ones—those other "frogs" who are too content, or too afraid, to stray from their preferred lily pad.

In any case, you mostly don't need to "hire"

PLAN B: FORGET PLANNING

"Ordering" enterprise activity is obsolete. And so is "planning" it.

Contention: We don't need—or even want—a "great plan." The days of "seeing around corners" are kaput. The "corners" of the New Economy are 90-degree bends that come every few breaths and continually reveal the most unexpected places

Instead of old-style planning, we need an entirely new approach to both preparedness and execution.

New definition of "preparedness": an adaptable and hyper-energetic talent pool, along with a floating, shifting array of temporary alliances.

New definition of "execution": ad-hoc WOW Projects, started on a dime and executed at Warp Speed.

revolutionaries. Odds are (very high) that you've got 'em already: role models ... existing people who actually exemplify a Brash New Way of Doing Things. They are lurking! Waiting to be discovered! Waiting to be listened to! Waiting to be taken seriously!

So what do you do? Seek 'em out. Let 'em loose. Teach these "lead frog" heroes a few (but not too many) manners. Make it clear-as-a-bell to one-and-all that ... They Are the New Way!

> **PUTTING (GREAT!) PEOPLE FIRST**
> The term *"lead frog,"* by the way, is a nice variation on another favorite term of mine: Talent! Indeed, so important is this theme that I have devoted the final chapter of this book to it.
> See Chapter 4: *"Boss Job One: The Talent25."*

They Could Be Heroes

How do we find these "Lead Frogs," these would-be revolutionaries, these diamonds-in-the-corporate-rough? The obvious—and true—answer: You find them in your "network." But that might not be quite enough.

You might also need to follow what I call the "flypaper" strategy. In other words: Induce these heroes to come out of the woodwork by laying irresistible, sticky traps for them. Here, then, are some ways to add a little "stickiness" to your Systematic Pursuit of Heroes.

Fair Game. Consider the tradition of "event marketing," typically used in the consumer-goods world. Why not do something similar "inside"—that is, within your company? Put on an Idea Fair, a "Bragfest," an

leadership

boss work

KICK-UP-YOUR-HEELS MANAGEMENT?
Here's the kicker to this new "boss work" model: You, the boss, don't have to do anything!

You've got an idea. Empowerment. Quality. Risk taking. Innovation. Whatever. To see that idea become something more than an idea, you don't need to "launch an initiative." Because, in any sizable organization, there are bound to be angry, "powerless" people who are *already putting your "new" idea into practice* ... perhaps at serious risk to their careers.

Your job: Ferret them out. Hold them by the scruff of the neck. Lionize them in front of everyone else in your organization.

As in: "Look at Marilyn—she's the one! She gets it! She's done it! And she's just like you and me!"

internal "trade show." In other words: a public and well-publicized occasion during which the "lead frogs" jump out of their pond and demonstrate their Weird Wares. Result: Other freaks are inspired to show their true colors.

To Catch a Freak. Start a monthly "New Economy Seminar Series." But instead of inviting the usual suspects ... the gurus *du jour* (like me!) ... invite a Genuine Freak from within your company to lead each seminar. Again: Freaks attract ... other Freaks. (Flypaper, remember!)

Just for Fund. Another powerful approach: Create a "play fund" ... a dedicated bucket-o'-cash that people throughout your company can draw upon in small doses to pursue weird, wild, one-off projects. In short: Show them the money—and see what happens. What usually works best is to define an "area of need" that is specific but not too specific.

ASK THE "EXPERT"

When he was boss of Travel Related Services at American Express, Lou Gerstner became intrigued by artificial intelligence and, in particular, by "expert systems" technology. He wanted to make something happen. Fast. Even though he was the Big Boss, he didn't issue an order. ("Go do expert systems now!") Instead, he established a smallish expert-systems "fund." Each grant was for a few thousand dollars. Anybody could apply. The grant process was simple—no-nonsense application, quick approval (or disapproval).

Only a couple of years later, according to Ed Feigenbaum (a great pioneer of expert systems and the author of The Rise of the Expert Company*), AmEx had an astonishingly high share of all the world's expert systems then in place! And the company had reaped millions upon millions of dollars as a result. That is, Gerstner hadn't "ordered it." He had, instead, concocted the stickiest of "flypaper."*

Bottom line: Gerstner didn't mandate all this from on high. Instead, he induced Weirdos to Come Out of the Woodwork.

BREAK THE QUARANTINE!

Here's another image that gets across the "find heroes" part of leadership: Think "epidemic." Think "infection." Think "germ theory."

That's right. Maybe you should study epidemiology ... if you want to become a Master of Culture Change ... if you want to start (yes!) an Epidemic of WOW Projects.

The big idea: Help and honor the already-"infected" ones—the ones who are too often shunned as disease carriers ... when in fact they are "carriers" of a New and Exciting Culture.

*How do you know if
an idea like "radical
sabbatical" is truly
radical ... and truly right
for you? Answer: Always
trust your gut.*

*Alex Trotman didn't
get everything right as
CEO of Ford. But he
introduced some Very
Cool Products. I once
read that he wasn't
happy with a new idea
unless it "scared me half
to death" (or words to
that effect).*

*That's a nice test for
the "radical Sabbatical"
idea. Or, indeed, for any
"radical" idea.*

Time Off for Weird Behavior.

How about setting up a special scholarship fund for ... Radical Sabbaticals? People could apply, much as they would for the grant fund mentioned above, for the opportunity to spend (say) six months with a Cool Customer or a Scintillating Supplier. Or maybe they would apply to work with a Profound Professor on a research project. Whatever. Call it "outside-the-company thinking."

Rules of Encouragement

The "lead frog" strategy. Laying out "flypaper." Whatever you call it, I know it works. The ultimate example (for me): the project that led directly to my writing *In Search of Excellence.*

When I was at McKinsey & Co., I was handed the reins of a two-bit project on "organization effectiveness." I didn't have much real power. But I did have a few ideas and, more important, a lot of passion. And by dint of that passion, I slowly attracted a passel of "powerless" youngsters to my cause. The ground was ripe for picking: McKinsey's "strategy-is-everything" emphasis had given rise to a crop of renegade youth. (Young-and-restless types: Every sizable firm has 'em. That's the good news. No, that's the ... Great News!) And so I searched high and low for them, using all of my friends' networks.

Hence the origin of what I like to call the McKinsey Children's Crusade. I'd like to think it did make the (management) earth wobble a bit—though "my kids" are all now long of tooth.

My "search for excellence" at McKinsey yielded a slew of insights into the art of "lead frog" leadership:

1. "Lead frogs" ... Upstart Practitioners of Cool ... are *always* with us.

leadership

boss work

2. Your job as boss: Find 'em. Excite 'em. Offer 'em a Revolutionary Peer Group. (And don't give 'em too much visibility too soon—you'll scare 'em off.)

3. After you articulate your point of view, your chief role becomes that of Community Organizer, Cheerleader, Provider of Camouflage Gear, and Chronicler-in-Chief.

4. "Lead frogs" tend to be relatively junior ... and formally "powerless." (Which is to say: The "system" hasn't licked 'em yet.)

5. "Powerless" is Cool—because, for the heroes among us ... "Powerless" means "Pissed Off," which in turn means "Prepared to Go for It or Go Bust."

The Way of the Demo

Heroes. Demos. Stories.

I won't say a great deal here about the second part of that equation. Quite simply, a "Demo" is an early-stage WOW Project. Demos are what your Heroes (aka "Lead Frogs") will do once you give them a green light. (Or maybe they've already done a WOW Project ... on the sly ... and your green light will give them permission to come out of the woodwork.) Demos are Exciting Experiments ... under-the-radar, on-a-shoestring, in-the-trenches efforts that vividly exemplify a New Way. Demos are the true "hard stuff" that sells and compels. Demos are ... Palpable Proof that Seriously Cool Change is not only possible—it's already under way!

Demos are what you tell stories about.

WOW POWER
How "Demos"—aka "WOW Projects for the Powerless"—percolate into being is a topic that I discuss at length in Essentials: Talent.

"GUARDIAN" ANGLE
Just as important as finding "heroes" is protecting them. All freaks need guardians. An inspired youngster (or, for that matter, an inspired oldster) needs somebody to keep him on the good side—or at least not entirely on the bad side—of the powers-that-currently-be.

At McKinsey & Co., I had Bob Waterman. During the years we worked together there, Bob probably spent 40 percent of his time protecting me from the Forces of Internal Evil ... the bureaucrats guarding the Conventional Way of Doing Things. Bless him. (And hey, Bob, I do know how much of a pain I was!)

Demos ... vividly exemplify a New Way.

The Work of Stories

"A key, perhaps *the* key, to leadership is ... the effective communication of a story." That's the "story," according to Harvard psychologist Howard Gardner, writing in *Leading Minds: An Anatomy of Leadership.*

That's a damn strong statement. ("Single most powerful weapon"!) And one that I wholeheartedly subscribe to. I'm trained as an engineer, not an anthropologist. (Never the twain shall meet.) But I've spent the last 30 years studying organizational change—which means that I've become a *de facto* anthropologist. And one thing you learn as a student of human culture ... whether your gig involves primitive tribes or corporate tribes ... is the (often unsung) Power of Storytelling. It was true in the bush. (That's all there was before written language. Go read Bruce Chatwin's marvelous book *The Songlines.*) It's true in the boardroom. And it's true everywhere in between.

What, after all, do leaders really do? John Seely Brown, former head of Xerox's fabled Palo Alto Research Center, puts it very simply:

LEADERS ...
MAKE ...
MEANING.

STORYTELLER-IN-CHIEF

The ultimate testament to the power of storytelling: presidential speeches.

Presidents who are trying to rally a nation to war ... must have a coherent, noble, and compelling story line. They must have a story that justifies sending American sons and daughters into Harm's Way.

To be sure, our obsessive attention to "spin doctoring" can cheapen the practice of storytelling. But the basic idea is right: A leader must be able to tell stories that cohere. Stories that engage. Or else he won't be able to lead dozens ... or dozens of millions ... into battle against the supposed forces of evil. The forces of bureaucratic evil, in the case of a junior executive leading a corporate training unit; the forces of life-threatening evil, in the case of a president.

"A key, perhaps *the* key, to leadership is ...
the effective communication of a story."

And what does "meaning" consist of? *Compelling* stories! *Coherent* themes! *Soaring* messages!

Those stories and themes and messages are about … you guessed it … WOW People (heroes, flesh-and-blood individuals) doing WOW Projects (demos, real projects executed on the front lines).

As I see it, an effective leader, as he/she makes the rounds at his/her organization, must ask one … and only one … question:

"GOT ANY GOOD STORIES?"

Stories … *are what animates our "reasoning process."*

Stories … *give us "permission" to act.*

Stories … *are photographs of who we aspire to be.*

Stories … *cause emotional responses.*

Stories … *connect.*

Stories … *are us.*

Beyond "Manual" Labor: The Armstrong Story

Back when we were working on *In Search of Excellence,* Bob Waterman and I latched onto a phrase that was popular at Hewlett-Packard:

MBWA: Managing By Wandering Around.

A fine phrase. A powerful, useful phrase. But my friend David Armstrong came along and decided to coin a phrase of his own. Armstrong, who runs a middle-sized manufacturing company, attended a seminar of mine,

SLAVE NARRATIVE: "THE BEST STORY WINS"

It took me an hour to find the line again, but it was well worth the effort.

I was watching *Amistad,* the Steven Spielberg movie about a mutiny on a slave ship. The vessel had made it to the United States; now a trial was taking place over the status of the rebellious slaves. Representing the slaves is black abolitionist lawyer Theodore Joadson,

played by Morgan Freeman; and advising him is former U.S. President John Quincy Adams, played by Anthony Hopkins. The Hopkins character asks the Freeman character to summarize his case.

The summary is brilliant, accurate … and wholly devoid of emotion.

Old Adams then counsels Joadson: "Early in my career in the law, I learned that whoever tells the best story wins.

What's your story?"

I was watching the movie on a pay-TV channel in a hotel room, and I had to replay the whole damn thing to catch that exchange again. I'm glad I did. Mark these words well:

WHOEVER TELLS THE … *BEST STORY* … WINS.

WHAT'S YOUR … *STORY?*

heard the MBWA bit ... and loved it. And then came up with this variation:

MBSA: *Managing By Story-ing Around.*

Now he runs his company, Armstrong International, according to the principles of MBSA. (And runs it quite successfully, I might add.) Stories, storytelling, and the technology thereof are the guiding forces behind How Things Are Done at David's company.

Armstrong began by actively trolling for stories. He urged and begged others to do the same ... and rewarded them if they did. (Call it "Systematic Story Seeking," a cornerstone idea.) Stories like: the youngster ... working, by herself and unsupervised, on a loading dock at 3 a.m. ... who went the extra mile for a customer. Or: the oldster in accounting who, without guidance, had cleaned up a mess brilliantly ... and salvaged a key client relationship.

Armstrong codified those stories and posted them—along with photos of the heroes—on walls throughout the enterprise. Then he turned the stories into a "policy manual." The only such manual that his company has. No baloney: The Armstrong "Policy Manual" is a storybook: a chronicle, in effect, of "How Things Are Done When We Are at Our Very Best as We Serve Our Customers and Communities and Fellow Employees and Suppliers."

Fabulous!

The point: David Armstrong took an apparently "soft" idea and turned it into a "hard"—that is, systematic and practical—management practice. And it worked. Big-time. (Not just at Armstrong International, either; David has started a movement of sorts, complete with books, training videos, and so on.)

The moral of this "storybook" romance:

STORIES WORK.
("MANUALS" DON'T.)
STORIES INSPIRE.
("MANUALS" DON'T.)

leadership

boss work

The Ultimate WOW Project? (A Federal Case)

My friend Bob Stone has a ... Great Story. He actually made a dent in the way the federal government performs. Following a career as an obstreperous (that is, loved and hated) change agent in the Department of Defense, he was chosen to be the Big Cheese of then-Vice President Al Gore's "reinventing government" (ReGo) program. No, the sun did not begin to rise in the west. But an amazing amount of unsung—and, truth known, often profound—change did take place on Bob's watch.

To the point of this chapter: Nobody but nobody played the Heroes-Demos-Stories game better than Bob.

Bob Stone understood, first of all, that you ... obviously ... don't "order culture change" in the federal bureaucracy. But the good news, as he also quickly saw, is that an organization with thousands of units ... and millions of people ... is guaranteed to be riddled with would-be revolutionaries. The real secret (again): *Find 'em! Unleash 'em! Lionize 'em! Induct 'em into a new Hall of Fame! Invite others, inspired by their example, to "sign up"!*

Stone offers a simple mantra that puts a whole new spin on the idea of corporate "culture change": "Some people look for things that went wrong and try to fix them. I look for things that went right and try to build on them."

Which is one reason I'd say he deserves the "job title" that he put on his federal-government "business card":

ReGo-a-Go-Go:
The 10 Commandments of Stone

In a marvelous book, *Polite Revolutionary: Lessons from an Uncivil Servant*, Bob Stone recounts his adventures as the federal government's top change agent. He asked me to write a foreword to the book, and therein I called it "the best book I've ever read on 'corporate' change." Here are the main messages I took away from Stone's saga:

1 **Talent Scouring.** The primary mission of ReGo staffers was not to create "plans" and "manuals" of their own—but to proactively ferret out heroes, eager change agents who had been hiding in their "dens" on the front lines and performing miracles despite the inertial or flat-out reactionary forces that surrounded them. Finding those heroes is no walk in the park; chances are they've been working "underground" for years, attempting to avoid scrutiny of their renegade ways. Stone learned to make end runs around recalcitrant insiders and get directly to the lead frogs. Such a tactic is especially important early on, when the shoots of revolution are tender—and skepticism or outright antagonism is running high.

leadership

boss work

2 **Field Marshals.** At the Department of Defense, Stone started a revolution where the rubber meets the road, among base commanders—real guys

---

EVERY PROMOTION TELLS A STORY

A great story has a smash finish. And what's the perfect climax to a successful WOW Project? A promotion!

When you make a promotion, you tell a story, whether you intended to do so or not. And a Page One story at that.

People watch promotions like hawks: Did the "suck-up" win? Or did the weirdo? How you, the boss, answer that question will send a message that resonates powerfully.

Consider doing what the military calls "deep dipping." Take a young hotshot who's stuck her neck way out ... and promote her up three levels ... at one leap. Believe me: That, like nothing else, will scare the hell out of the foot draggers and time servers in your group.

The Ultimate Demo: "Guys, meet your new GM, 32-year-old firebrand Sally Martinez!"

Message I: Never waste a single promotion.

Message II: The best measure of your Commitment (or not) to Radical Change is the Radicals You Promote.

(and some gals) out in the field. The farther away one gets from HQ, the greater the frustration. ("Headquarters revolution" is by and large an oxymoron!) Some frustrated commanders had put their tails between their legs and "retired" on the job; but the abiding urge to help real customers (soldiers and airmen and sailors and marines) brought out the renegade best in 10 percent of base commanders. These were Stone's Golden Ones. Their "real world" stories from the boondocks, once surfaced and circulated, packed real punch among their more reluctant peers.

3 **The "Call" of Fame.** Once he found his heroes, Stone was aggressive about putting them out-front—to give not-so-heroic types a whiff of inspiration. To see how this works on a grand scale, consider the people who get seated in the House Gallery during a presidential State of the Union address. These heroes are the dramatic, living embodiment of issues that are central to the national agenda. Forget the abstract idea of heroism: Here, right next to the First Lady, is a veteran in uniform; he exemplifies our Way of Life.

HERO.

4 **Awards of State.** Positive reinforcement remains the most powerful leadership device known to humankind. Bob Stone was a badges-and-baubles fanatic in a world where praise is especially sparing—the Federal Service. Mary Kay and the folks at Tupperware had nothing on the ReGo troops when it came to continuous cheerleading ... and to the doling-out of commendations of any and every sort. (As a Fed, Stone obviously couldn't toss out gajillion-dollar rewards. That may have been an advantage. His creativity in the arena of recognition provided stimulation and buzz that even a fat check can't match.)

5 **Project: Protect.** Some of Bob Stone's heroes didn't want publicity, even after he "discovered" them. Many were already at odds with bosses. So ReGo staffers learned to "watch" the bureaucratic "back" of such front-line change-mongers. Instead of a Federal Witness Protection Program, Stone initiated what amounted to a Federal "Heroes" Protection Program. Face-time with Al Gore, for example, kept a few heroes from losing their jobs. (It's difficult to fire someone who just publicly pocketed an Award of Valor from V-POTUS!) Another of Stone's tools: support groups. Pioneers need pals—like-minded souls to commiserate with and learn from. ReGo events and various networking practices helped here immensely.

6 **See for Yourself.** Stone got his first big break when he was appointed Deputy Assistant Secretary of Defense for Installations. In that role, he sought out "practicing radicals." To showcase their brave work, he hit upon (yes!) *demos*. Or, as he called them at DOD, "Model Installations." These were military bases run by those previously discussed renegades … places where people could go to observe "best (strange, new) practices." When Stone worked for Gore, "Model Installations" metamorphosed into "ReGo Labs"— Reinventing Government Laboratories. In both cases, the big idea is that we learn by example:

"Go. Look. See Cool Concrete Samples of the New Way … performed by … People Like Yourself. Go do your own version (only kinkier!). See: It Can Be Done!"

leadership

boss work

7 Fast Times at ReGo High. To the quintessential slow-moving organization, the Feds, Stone brought speed. His mantra: Move fast—before the Forces of Evil have a chance to kill you with piles of memos and endless reviews. He cites the dictum of the late John Boyd, an Air Force Colonel who said that whoever has the fastest "OODA Loop" wins. OODA Loop: "Observe-Orient-Decide-Act cycle." Confuse and confound the "enemy" by your speed. While the Champions of Inertia are busy scheduling the next "planning review," you swiftly get the job done.

8 Prominent Record. "Storytelling" sounds "soft" ... a far cry from the hard business of government restructuring. Stone demonstrated that stories are anything but soft. On the contrary, they are the ... True Hard Stuff. Stone did a masterful job of recording ReGo success through pamphlets, world-class videography, and so forth. Message: If it's not solidly and colorfully chronicled, then it never happened!

9 "Prop" It Up. Stories take on added potency when you deploy leave-behind props that illustrate graphically the Main Point. Example: the piles upon piles of hopelessly bloated federal-regulation books that Stone stacked behind Mr. Gore during ReGo photo-ops. (A classic Stone-ism.)

10 Terms of Office. Like any true leader, Stone understood the Power of Language. Some people mocked his insistence on using the word "customer" in the Federal Service—but that one little word made an enormous difference. In general, he changed the Federal Service vocabulary from "procedure first" to "service first." From "HQ boss first" to "field service provider first." From "adversary" (aiming to "score" against, say, a factory owner regarding OSHA regs) to "partner" (aiming to help the owner "get the right things done and create a safer workplace").

Zen and the Art of Culture Change

There's an implicit theme that runs through this chapter: indirection that even a Zen master would admire. We don't "order" change. We find the exemplars already lurking within our midst—and anoint them as Carriers-in-Chief of the New Culture.

When Jill Ker Conway became the first woman president of Smith College, she brought a bold agenda of change along with her. But despite her exalted title, she was trapped by budget shortfalls and a lifetime-tenured faculty that was not exactly chomping at the bit for radical change.

Rather than use her "position power," as the sociologists call it, to fight the extant culture, she chose indirection. On campus, JKC quietly asked around, found names of faculty and administration renegades, and began inviting them to lunch (thereby building her Fifth Column Rolodex). She also introduced them to one another. Thus the buzz began, and the seeds of a new culture were planted. Reticent radicals began to show their faces on the paths between the ivy-covered halls.

Ms. Ker Conway's outside strategy was equally ingenious ... and again indirect. Despite the fanfare surrounding her selection, even the board that appointed her was shy about dramatic change. Not true, though, of the many Smith alumnae, who were elated to see a *woman* finally in charge of this premier women's college. JKC devoted vast amounts of time to visiting with these alums, sharing her audacious plans, and seeking their support. In particular, she solicited "beyond-the-budget" seed money that allowed her to start testing her ideas for change. (Ah, demos again!)

Among this chapter's heroes, David Armstrong, Bob Stone, and Jill Ker Conway co-share the Grand Masters (and Mistress) of Indirection Award.

leadership

boss work

ORGANIZATION WOMAN

For more on Jill Ker Conway's leadership at Smith College, flip back to *Number 35 in the "Leadership50" (Chapter 1).*

The VC Model; Or: You, Bettor, Believe It!

Lurking beneath the surface of all of the foregoing is a Particularly Big Idea: *Think Portfolio. Think Boss-as-Venture-Capitalist.*

"Portfolio": a roster of "bets" that range from sure things with average payoffs to long shots that will make investors rich ... or poor.

All bosses are now, in effect, "portfolio managers." Or, to use a somewhat bolder (and hence more accurate) term: They are Venture Capitalists.

What do Venture Capitalists do? Two things. And only two things:

They bet on Cool People. *(Heroes!)*

And they bet on Cool Ideas. *(Demos!)*

The result: Cool Investments. *(Stories!)* Many of those bets ... most of them, in fact ... don't turn out. But a small number do ... and change the world.

The VC Model goes double if you're a Very Big Deal Senior Manager. You might think that if you run a Big Hunk of Big Co., things would be different. From that lofty height, don't you pretty much *have* to "order" culture change? Does the Heroes-Demos-Stories approach still hold?

My answer:
DAMN RIGHT IT

Say there are six vice presidents (or lab directors, or department heads, or division bosses) who report to you. My advice: Turn each of those half-dozen women or men into ... an avowed ... Venture Capitalist ... each with a clearly identified ... Portfolio of Investments. You should be able to pull any one of them aside in the hall and ask on the spot, "How's your WOW Portfolio 'performing'?"

(In other words: "Tell me some Cool Stories.")

In sum: *You, the Big Boss, are a venture capitalist; and each of your direct reports is a VC as well. Evaluate their "portfolios" constantly. And keep an eye on your own "portfolio of portfolios."*

In a Disruptive Age, that is the Essence of Boss Work.

STILL HOLDS!

BOSS DANCE

"If I could have chosen not to tackle the IBM culture head-on, I probably wouldn't have," former IBM CEO Lou Gerstner wrote in *Who Says Elephants Can't Dance*. "My bias coming in was toward strategy, analysis, and measurement. ... In comparison, changing the attitude and behaviors of hundreds of thousands of people is very, very hard."

Hence this chapter! The Heroes-Demos-Stories approach is made-to-order for changing attitudes and behaviors in the direction of swifter innovation; compliance with plans and policies (which are outdated before the ink is even dry!) is woefully inadequate—and in fact downright dangerous.

Boss Tools:
Toward a Scintillating WOW Portfolio

Once more from the top: Here are the sorts of steps I think you ought to take if you have a "mandate" to do "culture change." (Or even if you don't.)

1. Chat up people throughout your organization.
2. Develop a list of potential "heroes" ("lead frogs").
3. Hang out with those heroes-in-the-making. Find out what they want to change, how they would change it—maybe what they've already done to change it "on the sly."
4. Encourage them to "go for it."
5. Protect them when their bosses seek revenge!
6. Turn the "demos" of the new heroes' best efforts into WOW stories.
7. Showcase those WOW stories. Incorporate them into your speeches, your newsletters, your weekly emails. Add your public Stamp of Approval.
8. Promote one or two of the most illustrious heroes by moving them three levels up at one jump. (Now the "lead frog" is a leapfrog.)
9. Treat that promotion as a Big Story—as a recruitment tool for getting the foot-draggers to sign up and come aboard, or at least get the hell out of the way.
10. Keep the cycle going: more heroes ... more demos ... more stories.

Hint:
It never ends.

VC = VOCABULARY CAPITAL
New Boss Work requires New Boss Words:
   Hero. Demo. Story. Freak. Lead Frog.

Play. Playpen. WOW Project. Experiment. Prototype. Epidemic. Flypaper. Portfolio. Venture Capital.

These kinds of words must become part of your lexicon ... if you truly want to Create a New Way.

TOP 10 TO-DOs

1. *Stop giving orders.* Being the boss is no longer—if ever it was—about issuing mandates from on high. "Ordering" change is a *(stupid, stupid, stupid)* waste of time.

2. *Start offering encouragement.* The way to lead is to cultivate other leaders—people who will lead themselves toward Bigger and Better Things. Your job: Recognize them!

3. *Scout around your company.* Use every tool at your command (a "play fund," a "radical sabbatical" program) to lure and trap the "Lead Frogs" lurking within your company.

4. *Be "out to lunch."* Track down those in your orbit who are (seemingly) "out to lunch," and take them ... out to lunch. Find out what's on their mind. Mantra: The Freaks will inherit the Earth.

5. *Put on a show.* Give the would-be revolutionaries around you a forum in which to ... Strut Their Stuff. Call it a "seminar," an "Idea Fair," a "Bragfest." But in any case, *do it.*

6. *Protect and serve.* Be a guardian angel, and "run interference" on the naysayers and busybodies from the Old Guard.

7. *Make your promotions count.* Literally: *Count* the number of promotions in which you have influence, and then count how many of the folks promoted are ... Fabulous Freaks.

8. *Hone your storytelling chops.* Read a great novel. Take a course on the Art of Narrative. In short: Become adept at turning dry business facts into Stirring Tales of Achievement.

9. *Do something!* Take lots of risks, makes lots of bets—just like the venture capitalist that you are. Keep an active "portfolio" of people and projects, and keep it churning.

10. *Do nothing.* Once you make an "investment" in a project, sit back and let it "mature." You can't control the fruits of your "boss work," and you shouldn't try.

3

MEET THE NEW BOSS:
WOMEN RULE!

Contrasts

Was	Is
Competition	Cooperation
Rules	Relationships
Unitasking	Multitasking
Issuing orders	Asking questions
Rigid claims	Subtle cues
"Yes, sir"	"Thank you"
Conquest	Communication
"Management"	"Empowerment"
Command and control	Connect and cajole
Information: "need to know"	Information: "want to share"
Women in "support" functions	Women in sales positions

!Rant

We are not prepared ...

We acknowledge that **A NEW, FLUID WORLD IS EMERGING**. • But we retain our male-inspired, male-dominated hierarchies. • We "re-engineer." • But our way of thinking ... indeed our very vocabulary ("engineering") ... continues to be male-inspired. • We recognize women's "rights." But **we ignore women's *strengths***. • We value "toughness." But we fail to see that women's brand of toughness is far more "steely" than men's. • **WE PREACH THE VALUE OF A NEW KIND OF ENTERPRISE. BUT WE NEGLECT THOSE WHO ARE PERHAPS MOST FIT TO LEAD IT. NAMELY: WOMEN.**

!Vision

I Imagine ...

A WOMAN IN THE WHITE HOUSE.

A new epoch in which we all (men as well as women) **honor, reward, and take advantage of women's extraordinary strengths.**

An enterprise doctrine **THAT VIEWS WOMEN AS MUCH OF THE ANSWER** not only to the "talent problem," but also to the "leadership problem."

A WORLD IN WHICH THIS DAMN CHAPTER IS ... TOTALLY OBVIOUS.

Gender Mercies: Where the Leaders Are

Thus far, I've said a great deal about what leaders *do*. (They find heroes. They sponsor demos. They tell stories. And so on.) But ... where do leaders come from? Whence will arise the next great wave of much-needed Leadership Talent ... Talent fit for an era in which the very definition of "leadership" is being turned inside-out?

Leaders, of course, hail from all quarters. But my mind these days ... indeed, increasingly, with each passing day ... is on one (scandalously untapped) source of Leadership Talent: *Women*.

Great Talent is in short supply. Great Leadership Talent is in short supply. And the supply will get even shorter ... as the Age of Creativity and Intellectual Capital accelerates. And accelerate it will.

If we are serious about the pivotal role that Leadership Talent plays in the New Economy ... then the connection in all of our minds between "talent" and "leadership" and "women" must become automatic. The headline to a *BusinessWeek* Special Report from 2000 says it all: "AS LEADERS, WOMEN RULE: New studies find that female managers outshine their male counterparts in almost every measure."

My core argument here is really quite simple:

1. Talent is ever more important.

2. Our stock of leaders fails to match the changing needs of the time.

3. Women constitute a woefully neglected source of talent ... especially Leadership Talent.

4. Women and men are different.

5. Women's strengths match the leadership needs of the New Economy—to a startling degree.

DEEP END OF THE TALENT POOL
The extended "rant" that forms this chapter began as but one element of my Talent25 list. (See Chapter 4: "Boss Job One.") Then I got, well, pissed off. I decided that tapping the deepest well of talent would require nothing less than a ... *Revolution*.

Even so, my goals here are relatively modest. The "revolution" that I wish to foment is (primarily) an *Awareness Revolution*.

So: Listen up! Pay attention! Be aware! Ponder what follows!

leadership

women rule!

"AS LEADERS, WOMEN RULE."

6. Ergo, women must play a huge part in solving the "talent problem."

7. Accelerating the movement of women into leadership roles is a ... Strategic Imperative ... of the highest order.

OPPORTUNITY KNOCK-OUT

Sometimes, opportunity knocks. And sometimes ... it's a battering ram, and you just have to get out of its way.

My beat is business performance, not social justice. So I look at the issue of women and talent through a business-performance lens. And what I see, quite simply, is a strategic opportunity of the first order.

That opportunity is knocking ... and it won't wait very long for you to open the door.

The Helen and Judy Show

Authors Helen Fisher and Judy B. Rosener provide a powerful one-two "punch" on this all-important subject of gender and work.

It is a fact (damn it!): Men and women are different (significantly different!) when it comes to styles of perceiving and acting in the world. I've been studying this "gender stuff," frantically, for almost a decade now. And I am amazed by what I have learned. Books by the score have appeared about this topic, but those by Fisher and Rosener stand out for their ability to penetrate even a thick male skull like mine. To wit:

"TOMORROW BELONGS TO WOMEN."

HEAR THEM ROAR

Quick confession: I never intended to make the topic of "women and business" a centerpiece of my writing. It snuck up on me ... and then hit me hard at a seminal meeting with women business owners in 1996. I listened as one powerful woman after another described the tortuous struggle against male-dominated hierarchies that had marked her personal and professional life. Listening to those stories, frankly, made me feel like a spoiled brat (at age 54!).

Words like "epiphany" should not be bandied about lightly—but I had an Epiphany of Awareness that day. And it's taken root. And I am determined to ... pass it on.

(Please see *Essentials: Trends*, wherein I tell this tale in full.)

That's the unhedged bet that Fisher offers in *The First Sex: The Natural Talents of Women and How They Are Changing the World.*

Her argument, in summary: "On average, women and men possess a number of different innate skills. And current trends suggest that many sectors of the twenty-first-century economic community are going to need the natural talents of women. ... Women have many exceptional faculties bred in deep history: a talent with words; a capacity to read nonverbal cues; emotional sensitivity; empathy; patience; an ability to do and think several things simultaneously; ... a penchant for long-term planning; a gift for networking and negotiating; and a preference for cooperating, reaching consensus, and leading via egalitarian teams."

(Please stop and reread that. S-L-O-W-L-Y.)

"It's time for U.S. organizations to act," writes Judy Rosener in *America's Competitive Secret: Women Managers.* "No other country in the world has a comparable supply of professional women waiting to be called into action. *This* is America's competitive secret."

leadership

women rule!

BUSINESS WEAK?

It was 21 September 2004. A colleague of mine (a woman, it so happens) faxed me a copy of an ad for Cingular wireless service, along with a cryptic cover note: "What's wrong with this picture?"

The ad's tagline was "4 of the 5 commercial banks use Cingular for wireless email." Below was a pic of 5 folks—4 doing wireless email, 1 obviously not playing well with the others. It took me a second (I *am* a guy), but then I realized: ALL 5 OF THOSE FOLKS WERE MALE!

Just three hours later, I was reading *BusinessWeek*, and saw an ad for "The BusinessWeek 50 Forum." Listed were 15 "best of the best" speakers who would be appearing at the forum. And to a man (alas!), they were ... *all men.*

My reaction: IDIOTS!

Rosener's list of women's leadership strengths echoes Fisher's list:

- Link rather than rank workers.
- Favor interactive-collaborative leadership styles.
- Comfortable sharing information.
- See redistribution of power as victory, not surrender.
- Readily accept ambiguity.
- Honor intuition as well as pure "rationality."
- Inherently flexible.

(Again, please reread. S-L-O-W-L-Y.)

OPPOSITES, TRACKED

In Why Men Don't Listen and Women Can't Read Maps, *Barbara Pease and Allan Pease present an often humorous but deep-down serious look at just how … incredibly different … women and men are. Here are some items from the book that resonated with me:*

"Women think aloud. Women talk, men feel nagged."

"Women multitrack."

"Women are indirect. Men are direct."

"Women talk emotively, men are literal. Men listen like statues."

"Boys like things, girls like people."

"Boys compete, girls cooperate."

"Men hate to be wrong. Men hide their emotions."

It's a Women's (Work) World

Simply put, then: There is a set of attributes, more commonly found in women than in men, that match the requirements of the new world of … Value-Added Work.

Here's my own short list of such attributes:

- Women practice *improvisation skills* with much greater ease than men.
- Women are more *self-determined* and more *trust-sensitive* than men.
- Women appreciate and depend upon their *intuition* more than men do.
- Women, unlike men, focus naturally on *empowerment* (not on "power").
- Women develop *relationships* with greater facility than men.

One difference in particular throws a spotlight on why the New Economy favors women. Namely: Women are far less "rank-conscious" than men.

The Bedrock Rules of the New Economy:

1. Shout good-bye to "command and control"!
2. Shout good-bye to "knowing one's place"!
3. Shout good-bye to hierarchy!

Guys like rules. They like commanding and controlling. They like "knowing their place." They like hierarchical structures and the certainties associated therewith. (Hey, you can trace this instinct directly back to the cave.) Such structures exist not just because of "organizational needs," but rather because hierarchy

COURTESY CHECK
Women are relationship junkies. Men are not. A truism, right? But is it true? To find out, I conducted what might seem like a trivial experiment.

Over the space of three busy weeks, I took 21 commercial-airline flights. In each case, I had but one seatmate; among my 21 companions were 17 men and 4 women. I kept score of the frequency with which these seatmates uttered a simple "Thank-you" whenever a flight attendant performed some small bit of service for them (handing them a hot towel, serving them dinner, refilling a drink, and so on).

Here are the results: Among the 17 men, the total number of thank-yous was ... 11. (That's 0.65 thank-yous per guy.) Among the 4 women, the total came to ... 23. (Or 5.75 thank-yous per gal.)

So what does this "trivial" experiment amount to? You decide. I wouldn't touch a conclusive "finding" with a 10-foot pole. My "sample" was not statistically significant. (And I won't guarantee that I didn't miss a stray thank-you along the way.) But to me, the results of this little survey are ... Pretty Damn Suggestive. And, actually, not at all trivial.

and male thinking go hand-in-glove—and because men have always (until now) dominated organizations. But all of that is changing. The "organizational needs" of new enterprise are increasingly consonant with the female side of the "male-female difference" divide.

Male Trouble

Message to guys: It gets worse.

In 1996, according to an *Atlantic Monthly* cover story, there were 8.4 million women and 6.7 million men studying at American colleges and universities; by 2007, that disparity will have grown to 9.2 million women versus 6.9 million men. As a result of this extraordinary gap, we actually have more women than men these days in high-level math and science courses.

Almost everywhere you look, the numbers tell a compelling tale. (Yes, guys, *the numbers*. This isn't touchy-feely, wishy-washy stuff that you can brush aside with your "just the facts, ma'am" attitude.)

For example:

- Girls far outnumber boys in student government.
- Girls far outnumber boys in honor societies.
- Girls read far more books than boys do.
- Girls study abroad at a higher rate than boys.
- Girls outperform boys in tests of artistic and musical ability.

Yikes!

WHAT'S IT ALL ABOUT, ALPHA?

The male pack-animal mind-set is something that even a few men will admit to. "Guys want to put everybody in their hierarchical place," says Paul Biondi, of Mercer Management Consulting, with perhaps far too much frankness. "Like, should I have more respect for you, or are you somebody that's south of me?"

Hey, guys: Is there any possibility—any possibility whatsoever—that a woman could ask such a question ... and cop such an attitude?

Think about it. Please.

But don't despair, guys. We still rule in some areas. Namely: Crime and violence of all varieties. Alcohol abuse. Drug use. Diagnosed emotional problems. Learning disabilities.

BOYS WILL BE BOYS (UH-OH!)

Legendary organizational guru Phil Slater says, with tongue nowhere near cheek, "Boys are trained in a way that will make them irrelevant."

Change is afoot, and if you want to be part of the "relevant" response to it, you need to change accordingly. Thus, my message to men: Hire women. Promote women. But also: Learn from women.

Selling Point: All Men Out?

Okay, enough Sociological Big Think. What's the practical, actionable upshot of all these gender differences for your enterprise? How about this:

FIRE ALL MALE SALESPEOPLE.

I'm only kidding. Sort of.

9.2 million women

6.9 million men

TO A DEGREE: WOMEN SURPASS MEN
BusinessWeek cover story, May 2003: "THE NEW GENDER GAP. From kindergarten to grad school, boys are becoming the second sex."

Telling statistic:
In 2010, the ratio of female to male bachelor's degrees will be 1.42:1; for master's degrees, the ratio will be 1.51:1.

Note well: Degrees earned are the best overall indicator of an individual's future financial success.

FIRE
ALL MALE
SALESPEOPLE

I'M ONLY KIDDING. SORT OF.

Consider: "TAKE THIS QUICK QUIZ. Who manages more things at once? Who puts more effort into their appearance? Who usually takes care of the details? Who finds it easier to meet new people? Who asks more questions in a conversation? Who is a better listener? Who has more interest in communication skills? Who is more inclined to get involved? Who encourages harmony and agreement? Who has better intuition? Who works with a longer 'to-do' list? Who enjoys a recap to the day's events? Who's better at keeping in touch with others?"

That "quick quiz" appears on the back cover of the book *Selling Is a Woman's Game: Fifteen Powerful Reasons Why Women Can Outsell Men*, by Nicki Joy and Susan Kane-Benson. And, as you won't be surprised to learn, the answer to each question is ... WOMEN.

Now, obviously I don't counsel firing all male salespeople. But I do advise you to think, long and hard, about what makes for a great sales force. What qualities go into ... not just making "the sale," but making and maintaining the kind of ongoing relationships that yield ongoing sales success?

Several years ago, a senior executive at a travel services company approached me after one of my seminars. This guy, who had "made his bones" by selling systems at AT&T, got to musing about the Women Factor. "Tom," he said, "I believe there is a 'secret' to my success. Namely, hiring women." You can imagine my surprise. This was prior to my effort to understand the implications of gender differences in enterprise.

"My guys," he continued, "only wanted to call on 'Mr. Big.' But the women I worked with were willing to invest extraordinary amounts of time in 'wiring the organization.' They would routinely develop relationships several layers 'down' the org chart. By the time they got around to calling on the top executive, the deal was essentially already closed. It was eerie, really. Women 'did it.' Guys *couldn't* do it, to save themselves. I never really looked into the root causes of all this, but I sure as hell made a ton of money out of it."

The Reich Stuff: How One Guy "Got" It

From one conversion narrative to another ...

For some men, the path to recognizing the unique leadership talents of women travels along "the bottom line." For others, the pilgrimage is more personal. Put it this way: If a conservative is a liberal who's been "mugged by reality," then maybe a male feminist is ... a guy who's watched his wife get the short end of the professional stick.

Bob Reich is a former U.S. Secretary of Labor (1993–1997). He is also, according to one extensive recent survey, the second most important management thinker of our time. In 2002, Bob penned a book that outlined his views. The following excerpt, from a chapter titled "The Day I Became a Feminist," is one that I found absolutely riveting. It concerns the day that Reich's wife, a renowned legal scholar, was denied tenure at Harvard:

"A string of white males had been voted tenure just before her. Most had not written as much as she, nor inspired the same praise from specialists around the nation as had her work. None of their writings had been subjected to the detailed scrutiny—footnote by footnote—to which her colleagues had subjected her latest manuscript. Not one of the male candidates had roused the degree of anger and bitterness that characterized her tenure decision.

"Why? At first I was bewildered. I knew most of the men who had voted against her. ...

"Gradually, I came to understand. They were applying their standard of scholarship as impartially as they knew

RATIO AD ABSURDUM

In early 2001, in almost back-to-back succession, I addressed three of the world's largest financial advisory services companies. Operations at such companies fall into two big categories: service and sales. On the service side at all three of those firms, 80 percent of the employees (give or take no more than a percentage point or two) were female, and 20 percent men. On the sales side, the proportion was rigidly reversed: 80 percent male, and 20 percent female.

If you believe, as I and many others do, that women are better "relationship sellers" than men, then that distribution of talent is ... Truly Stupid.

how. Yet their standard assumed that the person to whom they applied it had gone through the same training and had the same formative intellectual experiences as they. It assumed further that the person had gained along the way the same understandings of academic discipline, and the same approaches to core problems, as they had gained. ...

"They had applied their standard as impartially as they knew how, but it was a male standard."

Reich goes on to explain how he has integrated an awareness of gender differences into his own work:

"The vice president of a corporation that I advise tells me he can't implement one of my recommendations, although he agrees with it. 'I have no authority,' he explains. 'It's not my turf.' Later the same day, his assistant vice president tells me that the recommendation can be implemented easily. 'It's not formally within our responsibility,' she says, off-handedly. 'But we'll just make some suggestions here and there, at the right time, to the right folks, and it'll get done.' Is the male vice president especially mindful of formal lines of authority and his female assistant especially casual, or do they exemplify differences in how men and women in general approach questions of leadership?

"If being a 'feminist' means noticing these sorts of things, then I became a feminist the day my wife was denied tenure. But what is my responsibility, as a male feminist, beyond merely noticing? At the least: to remind corporate recruiters that they shouldn't be asking about whether prospective female employees want to have a

leadership

women rule!

"RELATIONSHIP" TALK

"Investors are looking more and more for a relationship with their financial advisers," says Hardwick Simmons, former CEO of Prudential Securities. "They want someone they can trust, someone who listens.

... In my experience, in general, women may be better at these kinds of relationship-building skills than are men."

He says "women may be better ..." I say "women certainly *are* better ..."

family; to warn male colleagues about subtle possibilities of sexual bias in their evaluations of female colleagues; to help ensure that women are listened to within otherwise all-male meetings; to support my women students in the classroom, and to give explicit legitimacy to differences in the perceptions and leadership styles of men and women. In other words, just as I seek to educate myself, I must also help to educate other men.

"This is no small task. The day after the vote on my wife's tenure, I phoned one of her opponents—an old curmudgeon, as arrogant as he is smart. Without the slightest sense of the irony lying in the epithet I chose to hurl at him, I called him a son of a bitch."

Return to Gender: Toward a Talent Revolution

Moving women into the positions where they deserve to be isn't easy. Alas, few companies have even tried. One organization that has made strides in this direction is Deloitte & Touche. Douglas M. McCracken, former big boss at Deloitte, described his firm's "epiphany" in a 2000 *Harvard Business Review* article titled "Winning the Talent War for Women: Sometimes It Takes a Revolution."

Deloitte was doing pretty well in that "war." It was working hard to hire Great Women. It was giving them very high marks—higher than men!—in their early years.

And then … *the women left.*

Ah, you say: The Great Baby Problem strikes!

Not so fast, amigo.

"Deloitte was doing a great job of hiring high-performing women," McCracken writes. "In fact, women

A "LONG WAY"?
GO FIGURE (I)
Women, to quote the old slogan, "have come a long way, baby." But they have an even longer way to go. For instance:

As of a few years ago, women occupied *4 percent* of top management jobs

at U.S. companies. The comparable figure in Britain was *3 percent*. In the European Union as a whole, *2 percent*. And in Japan, less than *1 percent*.

And before you go thinking that U.S. women have "come a longer way" than others, read the

following, from *Closing the Leadership Gap*, a new (2004) book by Marie C. Wilson: "Internationally, the United States ranks 60th in women's political leadership, behind Sierra Leone and tied with Andorra." *60th!*
PATHETIC!

Women develop relationships with greater facility than men.

often earned higher performance ratings than men in their first years with the firm. Yet the percentage of women decreased with each step up the career ladder.

"Most [women] weren't leaving to raise families; they had weighed their options in Deloitte's male-dominated culture and found them wanting. Many of them, dissatisfied with a culture they perceived as endemic to professional service firms, switched professions."

Deloitte decided to do a "Deloitte" on Deloitte. It carefully examined what was driving women to leave the firm. And it discovered assumption after assumption that inadvertently blocked women's progress at Deloitte. For example, writes McCracken: "The process of assigning plum accounts was largely unexamined. Male partners made assumptions: 'I wouldn't put her on that kind of company because it's a tough manufacturing environment.' 'That client is difficult to deal with.' 'Travel puts too much pressure on women.' "

So Deloitte went to work on banishing those assumptions. The firm has not transformed itself overnight, but it has made a decade-long strategic commitment to move women—in much higher numbers than ever before—into its top leadership ranks.

And that, indeed, amounts to ... a *Revolution*.

McCracken's word.

And mine!

DOWN TO THE WIAR

Deloitte & Touche puts out what it calls the Women's Initiative Annual Report, (WIAR). I can't "command" you to read this invaluable document ... but I desperately wish that I could. So please ... race to the D&T Web site (www.public.deloitte. com/wiar/home.htm), download the report, and read it.

This is exactly *what a* serious *strategic* approach *to this issue looks like!*

A "LONG WAY"?
GO FIGURE (II)
Another entry from the "long, long way" file:

At the turn of the millennium, Susan Estrich reports in her book *Sex and Power*, just *63* of the top 2,500 earners at Fortune 500 companies were women. Only *8 percent* of partners at Big Five accounting firms were women. A scant *14 percent* of partners in the top 250 law firms in America were women. In medical schools, 43 percent of new students are women; 26 percent of faculty are women; but only *7 percent* of deans are women.

Again: PATHETIC!

TOP 10 TO-DOs

1. *Open your eyes.* Watch for the presence—or, more to the point, the appalling *absence*—of women in leadership positions.

2. *Prick up your ears.* Listen for the many, many ways that men and women are fundamentally, decisively *different* ... in how they think, in how they communicate, in how they lead.

3. *Re-set your sights.* Good-bye Command and Control. Hello Cooperation and Collaboration. That's the nature of work in the New Economy. And that's how women work ... naturally.

4. *Hire them.* Women make up a bigger and bigger share of the qualified applicant pool. (Sorry, guys. The graduation numbers don't lie.) So go where the talent is—before your competitor does.

5. *Promote them.* I'm against quotas. But I'm (very much) in favor of ... affirmative opportunity. And Women-as-Leaders represents the Opportunity of the Century.

6. *Mind your manners.* Women understand that leadership is about Giving Thanks ... as well as Taking Charge. Ask yourself: How many people have I thanked today?

7. *Fire all male salespeople.* And don't stop with your salespeople. Again: Only kidding. (Again: Sort of.)

8. *Redouble efforts to end double standards.* Do what Robert Reich did, and help women to uproot the norms that hold them back (norms that, not incidentally, hold their companies back as well).

9. *Assail your assumptions.* Do what Deloitte & Touche did, and systematically pinpoint where—and *why*—women are falling off the fast track at your company.

10. *Take pity on men.* They'll need it.

COOL FRIEND: Helen Fisher

Helen Fisher is an unlikely business guru. An anthropologist at Rutgers University, she writes mainly about "romantic love" and kindred topics. But her remarks below, made in connection with the publication of her book The First Sex: The Natural Talents of Women and How They Are Changing the World *(1999), are ones that every business leader must heed.*

* *

Women are naturally extremely good with words, and this skill is associated with the female hormones, particularly estrogen. A woman's ability for basic articulation, which is simply finding the right word rapidly, goes up in the middle of the menstrual cycle when estrogen levels peak. But even during menstruation, on average, women are more skilled with language than men are.

And I think this particular talent comes from millions of years of holding a baby in front of their faces, cajoling it, reprimanding it, educating it with words. Words were women's tools for millions of years, and indeed we now finally have a century where the communications industries are expanding rapidly and globally, pulling women into the job market.

* *

On average, when women think, they tend to gather more data and integrate the details faster. When they make decisions they tend to weigh more variables, consider more options and outcomes, recall more points of view, see more ways to proceed. ... Women tend to think in webs of factors, not straight lines, and so I simply call this web thinking. Men can do that also, but they're more likely to focus their attention, to get rid of extraneous data, to compartmentalize, and then to proceed in a more straightforward, linear causal pathway. For that I coined the term "step thinking." And I think that they're both perfectly good ways of thinking.

* *

Web thinking is good in the home, it's good for rearing babies, it's good for driving the car and making sandwiches and talking to the dog and feeding the goldfish and watching television all at once. But what's important now is that web thinking is needed in the job market where the new buzzwords are breadth of vision and depth of vision and systems thinking. And in a job market that is changing so rapidly, to have that kind of thinking is critical.

* *

We're still going to see more women gravitating towards those parts of the economy where their web thinking is rewarded. And I think we're going to still see men gravitating towards that part of the community where step thinking is rewarded and where men's spatial acuities are rewarded.

* *

The rise of women is going to be very helpful to men. ... It's going to bring in a more balanced view of work life and of opportunities, and enable those men who don't want to follow the very rigid male-male dominance hierarchy to chart different paths. It will provide more opportunities and more choices. I think that women are still going to make different choices and different opportunities than men will, but if women moving into the job market causes changes in the job market to occur that are suitable to both sexes, then bravo.

* *

We are now living in a world that is incredibly ambiguous. And there is good psychological data that women are better able to grapple with ambiguity because of their web thinking. ...

What's interesting about our projects now is they're not lifelong projects. You form a team with a goal and when the goal is over, the team dissolves. And then you form a new team with a new goal until that's over.

And once again, women tend to be more flexible than men. And that trait, too, is going to be rewarded in anybody who's got it, and more women have it than men.

4

BOSS JOB ONE: THE TALENT25

Contrasts

Was	Is
"Human Resources"	Talent!
People are "important"	People are everything
"People power" as slogan	People power as strategy
HR pros as paper shufflers	Hire to position a company for greatness
"Competitive" pay-and-benefits package	Excellent pay-and-benefits package
Talent "pays its dues"	Talent claims its prize
"Training" is a department	Training is an obsession
Filling "diversity" slots	Feeling the diversity imperative
Women lag	Women lead
A secure job with "potential for advancement"	A Great Place to Work!
Management via ordering-people-around	Leadership via developing-great-talent

!Rant

We are not prepared ...

We pay ever more lip-service to "people power," even as we cling to our long-standing penchant for hiring and cultivating obedient "employees." • **WE SAY THAT WE TAKE "TALENT" SERIOUSLY, WHILE FAILING TO TRANSFORM OUR ORGANIZATIONS IN A WAY THAT TRULY MAKES THEM ATTRACTORS OF TALENT.** • But now we must become obsessed about talent ... as obsessed about finding and developing top-flight people as the general manager of a professional sports franchise is about recruiting and training top-flight players. • We must understand that, in an age when value-added flows from creativity, **a quirky, energetic, and (yes) disobedient "talent pool"** has become the ... primary basis of competitive advantage ... perhaps **the only basis for competitive advantage.**

!Vision

I imagine ...

A world where **"attracting and developing talent"** holds as much sway for leaders of a typical Finance Department ... as it does for the GM of a Professional Sports Franchise.

A WORLD WHERE COMPANIES FOCUS ON CREATING AWESOME PLACES TO WORK— environments that exert a vacuum-like pull on the Best of the Best in every line of endeavor.

A world where leaders recognize that **talent** does not just "support" the brand; it *is* **the brand**.

Locus of Leadership:
An Awesome Place to Work

"Leaders Are Talent Fanatics," I wrote in Chapter 1 ("The Leadership50"). Now it's time to demonstrate just how ... *fanatical* ... I am on that point.

When I think about "talent," I think first of all about Bill Walsh—former coach, president, and general manager of the San Francisco 49ers franchise in the National Football League. I've known Bill for well over a decade, and he is ... a *Talent Freak*. Pro-football GMs like Bill toil away acquiring and developing the best 48-player active-duty roster imaginable, and they do it ... *25 hours a day, 8 days a week, 53 weeks a year*.

Talent *is* a 25-8-53 affair. That's obviously true for the GM of that 48-player pro football team. So: Why shouldn't it be (equally) true—in (exactly) the same way, and to (exactly) the same degree—if you're the leader of a 48-person finance department?

Why not? (Damn it.)

On the one hand, Awesome Talent has the freedom to roam the earth—to pick off the best gigs, to pocket the largest financial rewards. In that sense, organizations will increasingly take a back seat. (Think of how players have mostly ruled professional team sports since the coming of free agency. Or better: Think of how individual sports icons—Venus and Serena Williams, anyone?—are redefining "Talent" for a New Era.)

On the other hand, though, enterprises that manage to master the market for talent will do better than ever. (Think of how sports-team honchos shuffle and reshuffle their rosters—relentlessly, constantly—in order to lock in a winning combination.)

And to attract, retain, and obtain the most from Awesome Talent, organizations will need to offer up an ... Awesome Place to Work. A place where people not only get paid "their due," but also ... Get to Initiate & Execute Great Things. A place where they can add ... "Awesome Entries" ... to their ... WOW Project Portfolio ... and add Equity to their "Brand Called You."

alent25

THE BOYS IN THE BRAND

Talent. Brand. Leadership. *The players on a Professional Sports Franchise
exemplify the way that those ideas converge to form a single model
of organization excellence. Every player is ... A "Brand Called You."
Together, the players on the roster constitute ... the Brand of the Team.
And managing that roster is the Alpha and Omega of ... Leadership.*

Again: The same goes for a 48-person Finance Department.

*For more on the "Brand Called You" model of talent, please read the
companion book* Essentials: Talent.

The Talent25

Awesome Places to Work. Just as "individuals," "workers"
must re-imagine themselves as "talent," so enterprises
that want to draw in enterprising people must re-imagine
themselves as ... *talent-magnet organizations*.

But how?

My solution: The Talent25—a silver jubilee of ideas
for vaulting the "people issue" (henceforth to be known
as the "talent opportunity") from soaring rhetoric in an
annual report to ... Hard Strategic Reality:

1. Put People First! (For Real).

The phrase has rolled off many a corporate lip: "People
are our most important asset." The problem: It's mostly
been ... BULLSHIT. Subject of lip service, to be sure,
and believed at some level, to be sure; but not ... the
Essence of What Enterprise Does. Not ... the Essence of
... HOW LEADERSHIP SPENDS ITS TIME.

I don't mean to say that most enterprises ignore
the "people thing." Of course they don't. But there is a
special meaning to the word "first," as in "putting people
first." It means that "getting the people thing right" is
alpha and omega ... and every letter, Greek or non-Greek,
in between.

2. Be Obsessed.

About 20 years ago, we Americans went after the "quality thing" hammer-and-tong. We made enormous headway. Dr. Deming's Sacred Fourteen Principles had something to do with that success. But the real core of the achievement was this: *We put "quality" at the tip-top of ... The Business Agenda.*

If in 1975 you had sat down for a two-hour meeting with a cross-section of U.S. managers, "quality" might not have come up at all. Sit down with the same group ten years later, and half of the discussion would have been on that very topic. Thousands upon thousands of managers had spent 25 percent, and then 50 percent, and then often 75 percent, of their precious time on one thing: quality.

The most important trait associated with ... Mastery (of any damn thing) ... is ... *Attention.* Or: *Time Spent.*

If you're looking to ... Master the Talent Game ... there is a clear first step that you must take: PUT IT AT THE TOP OF THE AGENDA. And keep it there.

Pursuit of Talent. Either it's an obsession ... or you're not serious about it. Either you spend virtually all your time on it ... or you don't.

3. Pursue the Best.

If you are an unrepentant Connoisseur of Talent ... you will not settle for anything less than the best. In finance. In telemarketing. In the First Violinist's chair. You will leave a job open before you will "fill a slot" with a mediocrity. That goes for a managerial job. Or a telemarketing slot.

PURE REVIEW

When the "business review" occurs—weekly, monthly, quarterly—what agenda item comes first? Strategy? Budget?

I believe that the "people stuff" must come first.

Alas, all too often, the "HR stuff" is left until last.

That's not what ... WINNING THE GREAT WAR FOR TALENT ... is all about.

"PICKING" POINT

Shortly after Jack Welch retired from GE, *Fortune* ran an article on a handful of companies that had outperformed GE in the market during the "Welch Years." One was The Limited. Asked his secret of success, Limited founder Les Wexner replied that it had come when he began to take as much pleasure in "picking great people" as he had earlier in "picking great sweaters."

Great Talent is not very kind to those who can't pass muster. So do the people in your pool of Great Talent a favor: Stress them out a bit—but don't surround them with second-raters. Give them the best.

It's a big word: BEST. But it's one that can—and *must*—be used in the Great War for Talent.

A few years ago, Home Depot decided to shoot for the moon—to take the then-$20-billion corporation to $100 billion in relatively short order. To make this great leap, Home Depot concocted seven significant growth initiatives. Then-CEO Arthur Blank laid down the law: Each of these initiatives would be headed by the ... BEST PERSON IN THE WORLD.

I love that!
BEST.
WORLD!

For example, one of the seven initiatives involved international expansion. Home Depot pursued the very best, as they saw it, and ended up lassoing the COO of Ikea. Was he the best in the world? Who knows? But he sure is a ... Damn Good Approximation!

Okay, so you're not the Big Boss at Home Depot. In no way, shape, or form ... should that keep you from going for broke—from doggedly pursuing a BIW (Best In World) attitude.

You're the boss. Of a 62-person Information Systems Department. Or a 217-person Telemarketing Department. Or a 97-person Distribution Center. You want to leave behind a Legacy of Greatness. Well, my friend, your legacy is one and only one thing: the TALENT that you beat the bushes to find ... the TALENT that you train to get the job done. Boss of a seven-person unit? You're in the ... Talent Business. FULL TIME.

Mantra: "WE WILL NOT TOLERATE NON-EXCELLENT TALENT ... ANYWHERE."

4. Weed Out the Rest.

When a new head coach takes over an NFL team, he rarely holds on to more than a couple of the team's dozen or so assistant coaches. He has a new philosophy. He brings a new air of performance. And he needs new talent—in the coaching ranks, as well as in the player ranks—to pull it off.

UP OR OUT!

We think that this approach is as normal as hell when it comes to the National Football League. (In fact, we fans get irritated if the new broom doesn't sweep vigorously enough.) Yet we think it's as abnormal as hell when it comes to enterprise. Maybe such "play-it-as-it-lays" strategies were viable in a more mellow world. But in a world where competition is both increasingly unpredictable and increasingly brutal ... Only the Best is Good Enough.

In other words: UP OR OUT!

Is "up or out" brutal? On one hand, I suppose it is. It's brutal if you're a 26-year-veteran who has not been held to ... Serious Performance Standards ... for the last 15 years of his career. On the other hand, if you've got

talent, "up or out" will come as a boon. I've consistently observed that talent likes hanging out with talent. The Tiger Woodses of the world love to play against … The Best. (Mr. Woods wouldn't much enjoy a divot-covered afternoon on the links with me.)

When a new honcho comes aboard, must all the old gang be dumped? Of course not. But, often as not, that New Outsider comes into an enterprise that has let things drift … by allowing seniority or log-rolling to drive promotions. So, while the number of "newbies" whom a new leader brings in will vary, she should be given a pretty free hand in picking her "coaching staff."

MANAGERIAL CLEAR-CUTTING

Just how clean should a new broom sweep? Ed Michaels of McKinsey makes the case for an aggressive talent-turnover strategy. "We believe companies can increase their market capitalization 50 percent in three years," he writes. "Steve Macadam at [the forest-products company] Georgia-Pacific changed 20 of his 40 box plant managers to put more talented, higher paid managers in charge. He increased profitability from $20 million to $80 million in two years."

Wow!

FOR THE LOVE OF … TALENT

In *Organizing Genius*, their book on Great Groups (such as the Manhattan Project and Disney's first animation lab), Warren Bennis and Patricia Ward Biederman write that the people in charge of such groups evince one consistent attribute: "Leaders of great groups love talent and know where to find it. They revel in the talent of others."

I love that!

Another of Bennis and Biederman's Great Groups was Xerox's famed Palo Alto Research Center (PARC). A colleague of PARC founding leader Bob Taylor once described him as a … "connoisseur of talent."

I love *that*!

5. Focus on Intangibles.

When it comes to talent, what are you looking for? The strongest *arm* in a quarterback? The highest *grade-point average* in a would-be pharma lab scientist? Or ... something more?

By "something more," I mean those elements of a person that you can't quite put your finger (or a number) on. And my discussions with Great Leaders have led me to conclude that "something more" matters far more than "raw statistics"—whether you're recruiting for the San Francisco 49ers or for Pfizer.

One of the great tests of leadership maturity, I've come to believe, is the ability to deal with "the intangibles." To get over the pretense that "only the numbers matter." All the great sports coaches I know agree: *Attitude and Heart Rule!* You can compensate for a little bit of slowness ... with a lot of heart and attitude.

6. Change the Profile of "HR."

I have long believed that human resources people should sit at the Head Table.

Problem: All too often, HR folks are viewed (all too correctly) as "mechanics." Not as ... Master Architects ... who aim to ... Quarterback the Great War for Talent.

I've devoted my career to the "people thing." I DESPERATELY WANT HR TO *WIN*.

DESPERATELY.

Why doesn't it happen?

Simple: A FAILURE OF IMAGINATION.

TALENT FOR LUNCH

As a neophyte at McKinsey & Co., I was given a thorny assignment that involved some economic reasoning far beyond my training. Befuddled, I called an old friend who was a Ph.D. student in business at Stanford. Before I knew it, I was lunching at Stanford's faculty club with a renowned professor of economics and the head of the Political Science Department. They were bemused by the conundrum, and chatted up a couple of their colleagues. I'm not sure the client ended up with the right advice, but I am sure he benefited from the thinking of some of the Top Talent in the World—all because of my unwillingness to simply "do the best with what was at hand."

I wasn't born yesterday. I understand there are thousands upon thousands of pages of petty laws and regulations that HR "must administer." But that still does not excuse HR from ... the duty to *re-imagine* itself.

As leaders!

As *the* leaders.

HR: I WANT YOU ... at ... the ... Head Table.

So work to deserve that honor.

NAME THAT DEPARTMENT!

As a name, "HR" has one thing going for it: It's better than "Personnel."

I want a new title!

How about Talent Department?

How about Center of Talent Excellence?

How about Seriously Cool People Who Recruit and Develop ... Seriously Cool People?

Words matter!

So ... my dear colleagues in HR ... make your words ... matter.

---

7. Forge a Bold HR Strategy.

Just about every big company has a "strategic plan"—a voluminous document that is the offspring of ceaseless, obsessive deliberation.

Question: In your company's "strategic plan," how big is the chapter devoted ... explicitly ... to "HR strategy"? And how prominently is that chapter placed?

PERFORMANCE (UN)LIMITED

I did a little work, years ago, with Les Wexner's Limited Stores. Truth is, they are a pretty formulaic retailer. Not a whole lot of room for merchandising experimentation in one of their small shops. And yet I discovered that, time and again, the top Limited managers out-performed the (very solid) center of the herd ... by a factor of ... *three or four or five.*

TALENT TACTIC: RECRUITMENT

Every NFL team pursues a Formal Recruitment Strategy. We call it "the draft."

So why (I ask yet again) should there be any difference between an NFL team and a corporate finance department?

Answer: There should be no difference. (NONE AT ALL.)

Recruitment should be as "sacred" and intense for the "finance department" as it is for a ... professional sports franchise ... or a great urban center's opera company.

Or maybe I should ask: Does your company's "strategic plan" even have a chapter (or a section, or a paragraph) on "HR strategy"? Most plans that I've seen simply ... tragically ... don't

That's criminal. There needs to be one.

With teeth.

And bravura.

Bottom line: Your "strategic approach" to Talent is more important than your market analysis.

8. Take Reviews Seriously.

Okay, you acknowledge that the "people stuff" is important. But do you have a ... FORMAL TALENT REVIEW PROCESS ... one that you treat every bit as seriously as ... the Budget Process?

GE does. "In most companies, the Talent Review Process is a farce," writes McKinsey's Ed Michaels. "At GE, Jack Welch and his two top HR people visit each division for a day. They review the top 20 to 50 people by name. They talk about Talent Pool strengthening issues. The Talent Review Process is a contact sport at GE. It has the intensity and the importance of the budget process at most companies."

Welch retired a few years ago, but his sense of priorities remains as compelling as ever.

Look at your calendar: If "Talent Review" is not on it in big block letters ... then you are ... not serious ... about talent. (Not even faintly serious.)

CUTTING PEOPLE "SLACK"? CUT IT OUT!
Could integrity be "more important than ever"? Answer, in a word: YES.

The logic goes something like this: In a "sloppy" world, where competition isn't all that intense, where product life cycles stretch out for years, where the enemy and his tactics and weapons are known ... it's possible to cut people a bit of slack. But these days, we need the ... BEST. These days, we need to subject even the BEST to an ... UP OR OUT PHILOSOPHY.

To do so puts a special burden on you, the boss: If you're serious about "up or out," then cronyism and other forms of dishonesty regarding Talent are ... OUT. OUT. OUT.

I once worked for a successful software executive who told me that he devoted 100 working days (100!) to the evaluation process—two days per person, twice a year, for the 25 people who reported to him. He spent roughly one day of each two-day evaluation collecting data; the second day was devoted to an intense off-site, one-to-one review with the employee.

I was stunned by the number. And he, in turn, was stunned that I was stunned: "But what do I do that's more important than developing people? I don't do the damn work, Tom. They do."

9. Pay up.
Do I believe that offering people Great Pay will win the Great War for Talent? ABSOLUTELY NOT!

I believe the *sine qua non* is ... OPPORTUNITY. That is, the chance to shine ... to "Make a Dent in the Universe" ... quickly. To take home a World Series Ring.

On the other hand, if one *is* given a Great Opportunity, and one responds with Exceptional Vigor, then one should be ... Rewarded Accordingly.

"Technically savvy and innovative people," Peter Drucker told *Business 2.0,* "have become unbelievably expensive." "We value engineers like professional athletes," said Jerry Yang, co-founder of Yahoo! "We value great people at ten times an average person in their function." "Top performing companies," wrote Ed Michaels, "are two to four times more likely than the rest to pay what it takes to prevent losing top performers."

If there's one thing that pisses me off, it's ... a boss who complains about "high turnover" in the hotel's

leadership
the talent25

TALENT TACTIC: LEADERSHIP DEVELOPMENT
When my friend Roger Enrico left a top "line" operating job at PepsiCo to become the (mere) head of "Leadership Development," the buzz was that he was being "shunted aside." Not so. Not so at all.

Roger's next stop was ... CEO & Chairman of the Board. PepsiCo had joined the (very meager) ranks of companies that take Leadership Development ... VERY SERIOUSLY. GE, of course, is another. The Leadership Development "process" can be very disorganized. Or it can be the ... Heart of Enterprise Strategy.

So which one of those alternatives describes your joint?

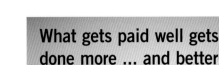

What gets paid well gets done more ... and better

housekeeping department ... and when I ask what the base pay is ... he or she tells me with pride it's 75 cents above minimum wage. "Housekeeping's not rocket science, Tom," the boss says. Well, housekeeping is "rocket science." (Great housekeeping, that is.)

I'm not arguing that every housekeeper ought to be paid $100,000 a year. I am contending that Housekeepers have more Guest Contact than any other set of human beings in the facility—and are, therefore, invaluable. And if they *are* "invaluable" ... and if "high turnover" *is* a problem ... well ... PAY THEM! If not that $100,000 a year, at least start them at $15.50 an hour.

Incidentally (not so incidentally!), when you raise that base pay, something else happens. Something Big. You

SOFT(WARE) IS HARD
Doubts still lingering in your head about whether Talent is "worth it" ... worth the money, worth the bother, worth this chapter?

Recently (2004), I came across a quote by Nathan Myhrvold, former chief scientist at Microsoft, that says it all: "The top software developers are more productive than average software developers not by a factor of 10X or 100X or even 1,000X, but by 10,000X."

end up attracting an entirely different pool of applicants. In the case of housekeeping, there is one "applicant pool" for $7.50 jobs. And another, quite different pool for $15.50 jobs. Q.E.D.

There's a famous old saw in management, and I mostly subscribe to it. It goes this way: "What gets measured gets done." But let me add a little something new to that old saw: *What gets measured gets done. What gets paid for gets done more. What gets paid well gets done more ... and better.*

10. Set Sky-High Standards.

I remember an old *Fortune* article about the best business-school professors. They had obviously turned their classrooms into ... Great Adventures in Learning.

The poll was based on student evaluations. Does that suggest these profs regularly delivered bushels of "A" grades to their grateful minions? Hardly!

With no exceptions, as I recall, each of these teachers were seen as "tough as nails." (Or some such.) I.e., being a "people place" does not mean running a "warm & fuzzy" place. People places ... Recruit Great People. Urge them to ... Sign Up for Great Quests. And then set ... Absurdly High Standards.

It's true in sports! True in the theater! True in ballet!

And there's no reason ... WHATSOEVER ... that it should not be ... routinely true ... in the Finance or IS or HR or Purchasing Departments.

leadership

the talent25

VIRTUAL REALISM

Foremost among the sky-high standards that serve to nurture talent is a ... firm grounding in reality.

Winning companies—and winning individuals—will be Supreme Realists. They will understand, for example, the power of the changes augured by the emergent software. They will embrace such changes. They will not avoid the challenges posed by new technologies.

Talented people will gravitate not to companies that promise "lifetime employment," but to companies that truly "get" the new realities of business. As a result, talent-rich enterprises will be marked by ... Unbridled Creative Realism.

11. Train! Train! Train!

In preparation for a speech to the American Society for Training and Development (ASTD), I discovered data that pegged the average annual hours in the classroom for the average American worker. The number: 26.3.

TWENTY-SIX-POINT-THREE.

26.3

THAT IS THE MOST OBSCENE NUMBER I HAVE COME ACROSS IN A LONG, LONG, LONG TIME.

We live in an age of "intellectual capital"—and 75 percent to 90 percent of what we college-trained white-collar workers do will be usurped by a $239.00 microprocessor in the course of the next ten or so years. What are we doing to become ... better and better ... more valuable ... and more valuable still? It sounds to me, based on the ASTD data, that we are spending a ... full ... *six minutes a day* working on improvement!

As I prepared for that ASTD speech, I turned lawyerly and kept a record of my own activities for three weeks in May 2001. I performed 41 hours of "work"—seminars ranging from an hour-and-a-half to seven hours in length. Life being life, I devoted 17 hours to what can only be classified as "other" (mostly petty bullshit, which dogs us all). And my "training" (which is to say, preparation) time ran ... *187 hours.*

That is, the ratio of "training" to "work" for the

FIT (ONLY) TO PRINT?

Peter Drucker writes, "My ancestors were printers in Amsterdam from 1510 or so until 1750 and during that entire time they didn't have to learn anything new." ("Drucker" means "printer" in Dutch.)

And now?

"Knowledge ... becomes obsolete incredibly fast," Drucker argues. "The continuing professional education of adults is the No.1 industry in the next 30 years."

Please note well what he is saying: Training (or, to be precise, retraining) will be the ... premier industry in the coming (many) years.

Strong words!

average worker is 0.01. For me it was 4.67. Almost a *500*-fold difference.

I'm not bragging. Not at all.

To the contrary, I believe that I am increasingly "normal" for a "creative-intensification worker." For a group of people who we typically call "Talent."

Think of "that word." TALENT. Think of its exemplars. Think about ... TRAINING. Can you imagine 26.3 hours ... per year ... for a ... diva ... violinist ... sprinter ... golfer ... pilot ... soldier ... surgeon ... astronaut?

OF COURSE YOU CAN'T.

Why is it?

Why is it ... that divas do it, violinists do it, sprinters do it, golfers do it, pilots do it, soldiers do it, surgeons do it, astronauts do it ... and only "businesspeople" don't seem to think it's necessary?

THE NEW BOSS: A "CLASS" ACT

Jack Welch, after cleaning up the wretched bureaucratic excess in his first few years at the helm at GE, turned to his special form of "empowering" people, labeled ... WORKOUT. Definition: Everybody was urged ... ENCOURAGED ... DE FACTO FORCED ... to "talk back to the boss." Talk back: LOUDLY. And the bosses were "encouraged" (FORCED!) to listen. LISTEN. INTENTLY. It was Welch's unique approach to training-dialogue-exchange ... in pursuit of Bullshit Removal throughout the Enormous Enterprise. Welch told his bosses they would ... PERIOD ... spend 24-days-per-year in the ... CLASSROOM.

If we are in the "employee development business" ... then the Big Cheese ... becomes Chief Talent Development Officer ... Chief Training Officer ... Chief Listening Officer.

Boss to the classroom, ear at the ready.

I think it's a disgrace, which is one thing. (ONE BIG THING.) I think it is going to catch up with us—as individuals and enterprises—which is far more important.

12. Cultivate Independent Leadership

Training should not be aimed at simply "increasing skills." Training should be aimed at fostering a ... *full-fledged entrepreneurial spirit* ... in each and every employee who works for us.

We *want* people ... EVERYBODY (I jest not) ... to "own" their piece of the action. Small piece. Big piece. Every piece. Training, therefore, should be training in "business" ... training in "entrepreneurship" ... and, yes, training in "disrespect for the way we currently do things."

DONE AND "DONE-R"

Related point: Training in "independent leadership" means training in ...Getting Things Done. Mark well these words by Larry Bossidy, former chairman and CEO of Honeywell International, from the book Execution: The Discipline of Getting Things Done *(co-authored with Ram Charan): "When assessing candidates, the first thing I looked for was energy and enthusiasm for execution. Does she talk about the thrill of getting things done, the obstacles overcome, the role her people played—or does she keep wandering back to strategy or philosophy?"*

---

13. Lead by "Winning People Over."

WHAT AN IDIOT! The "idiot" was quoted in the *New York Times*, as the recession reached its zenith in 2001. He runs a factory, somewhere-or-other, and told the reporter there was some joy to a recession: "Instead of employees being in the driver's seat, now we're in the driver's seat."

WHAT AN IDIOT! (Okay, I repeat myself.)

There's another fellow I know a little bit who's a "boss" ... the boss of a basketball team. He's won nine "world championships" in the last 12 years. Six in Chicago. Three in Los Angeles.

His name is Phil Jackson.

Jackson said, upon winning his eighth championship in 2001: "Coaching is winning players over."

Yes!

That's true if those players are Kobe Bryant and Shaquille O'Neal ... making millions. And it's true if those "players" are members of the housekeeping staff in a 300-room hotel.

Only "volunteers" matter!

Sure, the pay part's important. Sure, the person has to make money to support their kids. But World Hotel Championships ensue only if "they" ... bring the attitude of the volunteer ... to work ... every morning ... and thence turn that housekeeping department into a Scintillating Center of Excellence. (And I believe housekeeping departments can be exactly that!)

If that "housekeeping department" is a "Scintillating Center of Excellence" ... it will be because the "coach" (boss) "won players over" ... one at a time.

14. Reward "People Skills."

There are ... PEOPLE PEOPLE. And then there are those who ... Are Not. Institutions that Thrive on Talent invariably promote according to who has the BEST TALENT DEVELOPMENT SKILLS. PER SE.

I'm into what I do. Thinking about management. Writing about it. Talking about it. The analytics of "the thing." And the presentation thereof. To tell the truth, and I'm loath to, I'm *not* a ... People Person. I could not call myself, by any stretch of the imagination, a "Connoisseur of Talent." That's not what I do. That's not "my thing." And the only wisdom for which I will congratulate myself is the wisdom of realizing it! And not trying to fake it!

There are People People.

And there are those of us who are not.

TALENT TACTIC: LEADERSHIP TRACKING
I see it every time I visit the headquarters of a professional sports franchise. Of the many times I've visited corporate headquarters, I've seen it no more than ten times.

What is "it"? A Talent War Room— my term for the place where a team (or other organization) tracks its Top Talent.

Nothing is left to chance.

(Nothing = Nothing.)

If a Big Boss cannot tell you ... Every Detail ... about the Top 100 people... in his enterprise ... then he/she is NOT SERIOUS.

leadership

the talent25

Far too often, we promote The Mechanic (best trainer, best salesperson, etc.) into a leadership position because he/she *is* the best mechanic. (Accountant, salesperson, trainer.) Not because he/she is the best "people person." And yet leadership ... in the Great War for Talent ... is all about ... People Who Need People.

LISTEN UP: "People people" are not ... "soft." In fact, the best of them are tough as nails. Performance oriented—to a fault. Determined to collect the Best Damned Group of Talent they can.

15. Foster Open Communication.

If the "Talent thing" is all-important ... then ... TALENT ... MUST BE ABLE TO APPLY ITSELF TO THE TASK AT HAND. Which means that Every Iota of Bureaucratic B.S. that keeps "ordinary people" from talking to other "ordinary people" throughout the entire "supply chain" ... TO GET THINGS DONE FAST THROUGHOUT THE SYSTEM-AS-A-WHOLE ... must be eradicated.

Message: If one aims to ... WIN ... the Great War for Talent ... then we must ... UNLEASH THAT TALENT.

Barriers must go! (ALL.)

It goes without saying—though because it seldom happens, it must be said—that INFORMATION IS POWER. Hence everyone in an organization simply must know ... WHAT THE HELL IS GOING ON. In effect ... Everything That Is Going On.

Given the new technologies, and the enhanced pace of competitive change, people close to the action have got to be able to make decisions ... GOOD ONES ... on the fly. And ... that means that Everybody Must Have Access To Everything.

LINE EXTINCTION

"The lines that we drew on our neat organizational diagrams," write Frank Lekanne Deprez and René Tissen in Zero Space: Moving Beyond Organizational Limits, *"have turned into walls that no one can scale or penetrate or even peer over."* Erasing those lines will be Job One for today's and tomorrow's leaders.

BARRIERS
MUST GO!
(ALL)

16. Show Respect.

"The deepest human need," wrote the great American psychologist William James, "is the need to be appreciated." And the most talented humans—because they enjoy such a wide array of choices—will take their talents to places where they feel ... Most Appreciated.

Appreciation means many things. Opportunities. Financial rewards. Corporate awareness of work-family balance. And so on. But at the top of the list (bar none) is ... "SIMPLE" RESPECT.

Some institutions exude ... **RESPECT.**

Other institutions ... DO NOT.

We've all seen it a dozen times. (A DOZEN DOZEN TIMES.) You're in the presence of the Big Boss. He looks at you ... AND HE DOES NOT SEE YOU. He "sees" the next powerful person, halfway across the room. He does not see ... YOU.

The practical point? I think that we can "pay attention to 'such stuff.'" We can look for it when we *hire*. We can damn well look for it ... AND PUT IT AT THE TOP OF THE LIST ... when we *promote*.

In sum: Institutions that would ... "win" the Great War for Talent are ... Appreciative Institutions.

17. Embrace the Whole Individual.

Some places ... GIVE A DAMN ... about you as a ... Human Being. Some, all too obviously, do not. Caring about people as individuals is partly about the details of "programs": maternity/paternity leave, health care benefits, day care, tuition reimbursement.

All those things are important. And one should strive, I think, to be in the Top Quartile on darn near any such measure you can imagine.

But it goes beyond that. There are institutions that … CARE. Institutions that treat you as far more than fodder for the nine-to-five cannon. Institutions where top leaders (AND THENCE LEADERS AT ALL LEVELS!) go the "extra mile" … to show their concern for their employees' family and community concerns.

I believe it's clear … CRYSTAL CLEAR … that people are attracted to … and retained by … institutions that … MAKE THEM FEEL GOOD ABOUT THEMSELVES AS HUMAN BEINGS.

And one of the (BIGGEST) things that makes that happen … is an institution that gives off "good vibes" on the dimension called … INTEGRITY. An institution that's "out front" on ethical issues. Family issues. Community issues. Environmental issues. Product safety issues. Quality issues. And so on.

(Alas, I have no idea how to define "integrity." But … I KNOW IT WHEN I SEE IT. Some places make me "feel good" … on the … INTEGRITY SCALE. Other places make me … SQUEAMISH.)

leadership

the talent25

"FOREIGN" EXCHANGE

Years ago, a colleague at McKinsey & Co. was working with a Japanese bank. He was in Tokyo when he learned that his father was mortally ill. He returned home immediately, and, alas, his father passed away a few days later. My friend was at home the day before the funeral, when his mother informed him that there was a phone call from some "foreign person." This "foreign person" was the chairman of the giant Japanese bank, who was calling to say that his thoughts were with my friend in this moment of Great Sadness.

I'm sure that this "Big Cheese" had an executive assistant who prompted him to make the call. No matter. The point is: The Big Cheese did make … the Big Call.

18. Measure for Uniqueness.

Who understands Talent? Your kid's third-grade teacher! (*If* she/he is one of the good ones.) Teachers are ... in the Talent Business.

And when do we *love* that third-grade teacher who has taken charge of little Sally or Sammy? We're especially appreciative when she is not a slave to "teach the test." When she is one of the ... Glorious Ones ... who understands that each of our six billion fellow humans is ... Totally Unique. She treats each of her 19 charges as a ... Totally Unique Human Being ... engaged in a ... Totally Unique Learning and Discovery and Growth Trajectory.

Obvious, isn't it?

"Talent" is not easily categorized. (Make that ... NOT CATEGORIZABLE AT ALL.) Sure, we put a stopwatch on players who come to summer training camp in the National Football League, timing them in the 40-yard-dash. But at the end of the week, when we're considering whether they should stay or go, we treat them as ... Totally Unique Individuals. We measure the physical skills ... and then spend the remaining *98 percent* of our time on attitude, learning ability, and about 27 other *intangibles*. And then we make a decision about keeping them. Or not.

Measure them by a Standardized HR Instrument? UTTERLY ABSURD! And ... if it's absurd for the NFL ... damn it ... it's ... equally absurd ... for the kindergarten teacher ... or manager of a four-person training department ... or leader of a 68-person telemarketing department.

We are all unique!

One size *never* fits all!

One size fits one!

Period!

Back to the NFL, where it's ever so obvious: There are 48 guys on an active-duty NFL roster.

WE ARE ALL UNIQUE

Message: 48 Players = 48 Projects = 48 Totally Different Success Measures.

I have a term for believers in Standardized HR Evaluation Instruments: Jerks! (Sorry. I can't print the term that I really use.)

19. Liberate Women.

Often, at a certain point in my seminars, I will queue up this simple slide:

DO ANY OF YOU SUFFER FROM TOO MUCH TALENT?

"Of course not!" everyone in the seminar replies. There is, after all, a Great War for Talent going on.

So where do you look? All sorts of odd nooks and crannies. But there is one not-so-odd place to look. Namely: the Majority Group of the U.S. (and world) population.

Namely: WOMEN.

WOMEN ON TAP

Among these 25 ideas presented here, none is more important than tapping into that great storehouse of talent known as ... the female population.

See much more in Chapter 3: "Meet the New Boss: Women Rule!"

THIS IS A YOUNG PERSON'S CRUSADE.

20. Honor Youth.

The new technologies are not out of their diapers. In fact, one can see a parade of technology revolutions across the horizon ... for years and years ... to come.

And who will lead this parade?

The 50-year-olds?

Hardly!

From an article in the *Economist:* "Why focus on these late teens and twentysomethings?" Because they are the first young who are both in a position to change the world, and are actually doing so. ... For the first time in history, children are more comfortable, knowledgeable, and literate than their parents about an innovation central to society. The Internet has triggered the first industrial revolution in history to be led by the young."

Innovation guru Michael Schrage calls "all this" the Age of Ageism: "The real innovator's dilemma isn't the threat of 'disruptive technologies'; it's the relentless rise of the quasi-adolescents who wield them."

I turned 60 a couple of years ago. Should all 60-year-olds be sent out to sea? For good? Perhaps not. Although I think I should honestly say, "Not clear."

GENERATION GAFFE?

I was reading a Special Report in Time *magazine about new handheld devices. I turned to my wife and said, "You know, the truth is, I don't really need any of this."*

Her wonderful response: "You really are getting older, aren't you?"

Well. Damn it. I was right. A 49-cent notepad does a much better job—for me—of keeping addresses than the latest souped-up Palm.

No, I don't need any of this. But ... my kids do!

They don't "want" it. They "need" it.

I *will* say, and I do routinely:

THIS IS A YOUNG PERSON'S CRUSADE.

I am curious. But the most curious person I know is 33 years my senior. Namely, my mom, age 95. So I believe that we "old farts" can be curious as the dickens.

But that's not the point. There is something that I ... *cannot* ... be. Namely: *naïve!* The great physicist and Nobel Laureate Richard Feynman said it was no

leadership

the talent25

coincidence that virtually all major discoveries in physics were made by those under the age of 25. Here's why: When you're under 25, Feynman concluded, you don't know what you don't know.

I won't let my kids near my computer! The reason: They are too good. They're always trying this. Trying that. Stretching its capability to the utmost.

They are members of a ... New Species. In fact, the youngster in Tokyo, born (it would seem) with a game console in his hand, is said to belong to the "thumb generation." That is, having used their thumbs on the game consoles so much, they now use their thumbs to perform many acts that the rest of us use our index finger for ... turning on light switches and the like.

A dozen dozen stories like this are available. And they all add up to one thing:

YOUTH WILL DOMINATE THIS NEW TECHNOLOGY. Which means:

YOUTH WILL DOMINATE THE NEW ECONOMY.

FRIENDLY USERS

Kids! They take to new technologies ... instinctively. Dr. Sugata Mitra, of NIIT in New Delhi, describes a mind-boggling experiment performed in 1999. Personal computers were placed in kiosks in public spaces in Delhi. Because of the perpetual dust storms in the streets, they were made especially user-unfriendly courtesy of plastic covers on the keyboard. Hardly inviting!

Yet the young, computer-illiterate street urchins would approach the computers with glee. (The computers displayed English. The kids spoke Hindi.) The average time that elapsed between a kid's initial confrontation with the computer and his somehow getting onto the Internet and beginning to surf was ... eight minutes!

Thence I offer you my ...

ACID TEST I: How many members of your Board of Directors are under the age of ... thirty-five?

Thirty?

Twenty-five?

ACID TEST II: When was the last time your executive committee spent a full day off-site with someone under the age of ... twenty-five?

Thumb Generation.

Among the New Youth entering the World's Work Force, we are discovering—praise be!—a New Attitude. And it's an attitude that is not likely to be quashed, for more than a whisker of time, by the uncertainties of the current economy. Those uncertainties are, after all, directly driven by the chaos/mess associated with introducing so many ... Truly Transforming Technologies ... at once.

It is the Age of Intellectual Capital. It is the Age of Curiosity Rewarded. (Rather than ... Compliance Demanded.) We need people who, from the start, will ... Talk Back. Who are ... Determined to Get Ahead ... fast. Who are ... Unimpressed ... by the recalcitrance of the corporate bureaucracies they run up against. Who are determined to ... Make a Dent in the Universe. Who are determined ... to stick their shiv between my aging and brittle ribs.

Bless them!

May these Youthful Revolutionaries overturn us with great dispatch!

THIRTY-FIVE? **THIRTY?**

21. Create Opportunities to Lead.

It's so obvious, I shouldn't have to say it (but I do): THE
WAY TO CREATE LEADERS IS TO ... LET PEOPLE LEAD.

You find somebody great.

Terrific.

Put that somebody in charge.

Of *something*.

Right now.

The average complex project has task upon task upon
task. Sub-task upon sub-task upon sub-task.

Translation: ENORMOUS NUMBERS OF ...
LEADERSHIP OPPORTUNITIES.

Use those opportunities. Divide the project into a
bushel of sub-tasks. Find a "kid" with a bit of spirit—and
a lot more smarts, relative to the new technologies, than
you and I have—and put her in charge.

So she's 23? SO WHAT?

LEADING IS NOT ABOUT AGE.

**THE PEPSI
(RE)GENERATION**
At smart companies, fast
tracking of top talent is
the norm. Back in my
hard-core consulting days,
I particularly enjoyed
working with PepsiCo. Near
the top of the reasons why:
THOSE WHO PERFORM
INCREDIBLY WELL ... GET
AHEAD ... INCREDIBLY FAST.
It's Pepsi-normal to find
someone age 30 running a
billion-dollar brand.

PepsiCo's message: If
you do ... DAMN WELL ...
then you will ... get ahead
... DAMN FAST.

TWENTY-FIVE?

Ed Michaels of McKinsey & Co. presents a list of "demands" that Gen-X talent is making of companies today. (Even after the dot.com crash.)

These rising stars ...

- Love the challenge.
- Want responsibility early.
- Crave freedom, independence, and control.
- Are obsessed with building their personal human capital.
- Value more than work.
- See a very compressed career timeline.

MENTOR HEALTH SYSTEM

Fact: It's a New World, marked by New Rules.

Fact: We need to "bring people along" ... far faster than before.

Fact: Fast ascendants need ... HELP.

Best definition of help: MENTORS.

I want the young to race ahead! Thence "oldsters" may discover a new definition of their "excellence." Such "excellence" will no longer be "wise decision making," but ... DEVELOPING THE YOUNG.

I'm older than you are. (Statistically, the odds are clear in that regard.)

When one gets "old," one realizes that the greatest contribution one can make is to ... DEVELOP OTHERS.

In a word: MENTOR. If you really believe in the Great War for Talent, then ... CHERISH MENTORING.

Go one step further: MEASURE SENIOR LEADERS IN TERMS OF THEIR MENTORING SKILLS TRACK RECORD.

GET OVER IT

You think these youngsters are getting ahead of themselves?

Get over it.

"Talented people," Michaels writes, "are less likely to wait their turn. We used to view young people as 'trainees'; now they are authorities. Arguably this is the first time the older generation can—and must—leverage the younger generation very early in their careers."

22. Relish Diversity.

I am a New Economy Fanatic. Thence a Creativity Fanatic. Thence an Intellectual-Capital Fanatic. Thence ... a ... DIVERSITY FANATIC.

Does that mean I'm an Affirmative Action fanatic? Not necessarily. And in any case, that's beside the point.

What is the point? It's really quite simple: Creativity and Great Leaps Forward come from ... mix/match/mess. That is, all kinds of people providing all kinds of ideas that crazily bounce against one another ... and cause a lot of chaos ... and eventually cause a Great Idea to emerge ... which ... Changes the World.

BusinessWeek, August 2002: "Hiring diverse, even eccentric people, mixing them up in unexpected ways, and asking them to do something unusual can prompt surprising ideas."

"Where do good new ideas come from?" asked Nicholas Negroponte, founding chairman of MIT Media Lab. "That's simple ... from differences. Creativity comes from unlikely juxtapositions. The best way to maximize differences is to mix ages, cultures, and disciplines."

Carnegie-Mellon professor Richard Florida writes in a similar vein about the regional accumulation of "creative capital": "You cannot get a technologically innovative place unless it's open to weirdness, eccentricity, and difference."

So "diversity" means "big deal stuff"—the lifeblood of nations.

leadership

the talent25

BusinessWeek, August 2002: "The coming battle for immigrants: the ability to absorb foreigners could determine whether nations in the industrialized world will grow or stagnate."

HIP, HIP HYBRID!

Diversity means lots of things. BIG THINGS. Senior Wall Street Journal *writer G. Pascal Zachary penned a magnificent book,* The Global Me: New Cosmopolitans and the Competitive Edge, *in 2000. "Diversity defines the health and wealth of nations in the new century," Zachary writes. "Mighty is the mongrel. ... The hybrid is hip. ... The impure, the mélange, the adulterated, the blemished, the rough, the black-and-blue, the mix-and-match—these people are inheriting the earth. Mixing is the new norm. ... Mixing trumps isolation. It spawns creativity, nourishes the human spirit, spurs economic growth, and empowers nations."*

Talk about strong language!

But Zachary is just warming up:

"Capitalism and the conditions for creating wealth have changed in ways that play to the strengths of hybrid individuals, organizations, and nations. And those that wish to profit from changing economic conditions must view hybridity as their first and best option. This bold claim warrants an explanation. The ability to apply knowledge to new situations is the most valued currency in today's economy. Highly creative people ... are misfits on some level. They tend to question accepted views and consider contradictory ones. This appreciation defines the mongrel mentality. Strangers instinctively question things that natives take for granted. Many things strike them as odd or stupid."

Diversity also means, I believe, "a poet in every accounting department." My favorite character in Silicon Valley's long-running drama is Steve Jobs. Time and again he's turned out incredible products ... that change our ... View of the World. There are many reasons, to be sure, for that extraordinary record of success. But a significant part of the story is that Steve has always loaded product development teams with all sorts of ... Seriously Cool & Seriously Weird People from Seriously Cool & Seriously Weird Places. "Expose yourself to the best things humans have done," he once wrote, "and then try to bring those things into what you are doing." Such was his explanation for stacking teams with artists, actors, poets, musicians ... and any other Intriguing Kind of "Weirdos"/"Creatives" ... who looked at the world through a different lens.

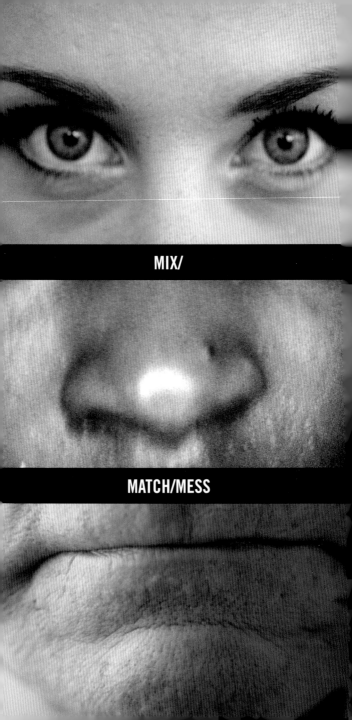

MIX/

MATCH/MESS

Diversity, then, is a strategic issue, and an encompassing one, right at the heart of future economic success—for the corporation and the entire nation. Political correctness? Forget it! Diversity's case is about survival—or extinction—in a Brave New World.

THE SEVEN LIVELY "SMARTS"

Diversity isn't just a "good idea." It's a defining attribute of … the human brain. Drawing on three decades of research, Harvard Education School professor Howard Gardner developed the concept of MI, or Multiple Intelligences. There are, Gardner argues, at least seven formal, measurable varieties of intelligence: logical-mathematical, linguistic, spatial, musical, kinesthetic, interpersonal, and intrapersonal. Each variety has unique value in terms of framing the world.

The problem? Virtually all of our educational efforts, as well as our company hiring and promotional systems, focus on "logical-mathematical" intelligence, perhaps allowing "linguistic" intelligence to sneak in the side door. We thus end up discarding—NOT AN EXAGGERATION—five out of seven varieties of human intelligence.

The result: multiple stupidities!

---

23. Celebrate the Weird Ones.

The Northern California psychiatrist's bumper sticker read, "The Cracked Ones Let in the Light." "Deviance tells the story of every mass market ever created," wrote successful tech gurus and entrepreneurs Ryan Matthews and Watts Wacker. "What starts out weird and dangerous becomes America's next big corporate payday. So are you looking for the next mass-market idea? It's out there … way out there." "Our business," said the great ad man David Ogilvy, "needs massive transfusions of talent. And talent, I believe, is most likely to be found among nonconformists, dissenters, and rebels."

Let's stick with Ogilvy for a moment. You rebut his assertion, reminding me that he was an "ad man." He's talking about the 'creatives' in the ad agency, you say. Perhaps he was. But I don't think that fact makes a bit of difference. In the new world of Creativity-as-Value-Added, we need "radicals" in every nook and cranny and crevice of every enterprise. Radicals … in Finance. Radicals … in Training. Radicals … in Purchasing.

Radicals … in Logistics. Radicals … in HR. Radicals … under every bench. Radicals … clinging like bats to the rafters. Radicals: People who don't buy today's act! People who are disrespectful! People who are bent on inventing a new act!

So what do we do?

Embrace (not just "tolerate") their contrarian points of view!

Here's a starting tip: *Quit looking under the lampposts where you've always looked before!* Quit hiring from the same-damn-schools … even if they are "great" schools.

You want freaks? (YOU DO.) You want weird? (YOU DO.) Answer: Obvious. Look in Weird & Freaky places. Hire from offbeat places. Hire offbeat backgrounds.

Message: Never hire anyone without an … aberration in their background. If they've been "normal" since birth, even "brilliantly" normal, don't expect them to do something Strange and Cool and Wacky tomorrow morning. Once a toe-er of lines, always a toe-er of lines.

I've often said to seminar audiences: "Never hire anyone with a 4.0 grade-point average." Sounds outrageous. And, of course, it offends a sizeable number of participants—who have invested time and money galore spurring their kids on toward 4.0 GPAs. Of course I'm not against intelligence. But a 4.0 average means: absolutely, positively … no time … whatsoever … for screwing around.

COOKIE MONSTER

Years ago I recruited for a Public Policy program at Stanford's business school. I did a quick first pass through several hundred applications, and only one popped out as a "must (under any circumstances) have." Don't get me wrong: Every kid was bright as blazes. But this fellow had also organized a team that ended up making it, as I recall, into the *Guinness Book of World Records*. He and his campus colleagues

had baked a one-ton cookie—apparently the biggest ever at the time.

I desperately wanted this person … because he'd done something Weird and Wacky, in a World-Class Way. I figured, if you've "done" Wacky-Weird in the past … well, then the odds go way-way up that you'll do it again in the future.

For me, that Cookie Man has become a metaphor. I exhort one and all:

"Find the One-Ton Cookie Freaks!"

do any of you suffer from too much talent?

If you have a habit of challenging the rules, it will probably emerge by about age eight. And if you don't have it by age eight, or at least age 18, it probably won't show up by age 88.

Find the aberrant ones! Embrace them! Reap the rewards of their offbeat behavior!

24. Provide a Setting for Adventure.

"The challenge for IBM, AT&T, and other mainstream companies," wrote AT&T HR exec Burke Stinson, "is to re-instill a sense of adventure in recruits." Great!

But to get from here to there is not easy. Perhaps we should begin by shifting fundamental "management" logic: Perhaps the Main Idea becomes "What can 'we' do for 'them'?" rather than "What can 'they' do for 'us'?"

"Firms," writes career guru Tim Hall, "will not 'manage employees' careers' … They will provide opportunities … to enable the employee to develop identity and adaptability and thus be in charge of his or her own career."

Bottom line: Talent-obsessed leaders are in the … Adventure Creation Business. Full time.

Why are people unexcited about coming to work?

25. Fuel Enthusiasm.

The chief goal of leadership, I have argued, is to engage people in "Voyages of Mutual Discovery." To do that requires an environment that is marked above all by ... ENERGY & ENTHUSIASM. An environment that ... positively vibrates.

Does your company attract Great Talent (remember: *Heroes*), people who will drive WOW Projects (remember: *Demos*)—that is, extraordinary experiments that you, The Leader, will use to inspire others (remember: *Stories*).

Why are people excited about coming to work? Why are people unexcited about coming to work?

Decent pay is one thing. Good benefits are another. (Both are Big Things.)

But the bottom-line is this: IS YOUR COMPANY A GREAT PLACE TO WORK? IS IT COOL?

MUSIC TO MY EARS
Management guru Ben Zander, also the renowned conductor of the Boston Philharmonic, describes himself as a "dispenser of enthusiasm."
BRAVO!

"CAUSE": WE LIKE IT
Winning companies, argues strategy guru Gary Hamel, "create a 'cause,' not a 'business.' "
By the same token, winning leaders lure Great Talent by offering not just a job, but an Aura of Passionate Engagement.

TOP 10 TO-DOs

1. *Pursue* ... Make the pursuit of top-flight talent your Number One Priority. Actively, aggressively seek out people for your company—or for your project team—who meet the BIW (Best in World) standard.

2. *Recruit* ... Look at your calendar. Have you marked off large chunks of quality time for the sole, express purpose of recruiting top talent? If not, do so. Now.

3. *Cut* ... Remove from your ranks those who don't measure up. Do it as charitably as possible, but do it with a ruthless focus on the needs of your Most Talented People. (They deserve no less.)

4. *Reinvent* ... Subject your HR department to the extreme makeover that it deserves. Rename the department, if need be. Whatever you do, turn it into a center of *strategic* impact.

5. *Build* ... Create a Leadership Center—a place where the development of leadership talent falls within the inescapable purview of Top Management. (If you don't build it, "they" won't come.)

6. *Destroy* ... Break down *(all)* barriers to communication. Your job as leader: Create the shortest distance between ... Two Top Talents.

7. *Review* ... Again, it's all about Time Spent. That goes for performance reviews, too. Make them a Calendar-Controlling Event.

8. *Unleash* ... Let loose the Weird Ones. Hire with an eye to Aberrant Behavior. (Tip: Scour résumés for "One-Ton Cookie Freaks.")

9. *Pay* ... Put your money where your talent is. Review your compensation profile, and make sure that you're not cutting corners in the wrong places. Mantra: What gets paid well gets done well.

10. *Inspire* ... Launch a Great Quest, and the Heroes of that Quest will arrive in its wake. Great People are drawn to Great Challenges. So: Set sky-high standards!

INDEX

AUTHOR'S ACKNOWLEDGMENTS

It required a far-flung virtual village to make this book. Here I wish to note a few "essential" residents of that village:

Michael Slind, editor, and Jason Godfrey, designer, both continued the sterling work that helped make my previous book (*Re-imagine!*) so sharply compelling. In adapting that book to make this one, they both achieved the noble feat of reinventing the project from within.

Stephanie Jackson, of Dorling Kindersley, pushed and pushed—and charmed and charmed—this book into being. Also at DK, Peter Luff used his sense of visual panache to help produce a "small" book with big impact, and Dawn Henderson applied her editorial talent deftly, creatively, and crucially at every stage of the project.

Erik Hansen served in his usual role of "project manager," though that term fails to capture the unique mix of doggedness and nimbleness that he brings to all of my publishing ventures. Cathy Mosca attended to details of authorial execution and factual accuracy with her typical vigilance.

My thanks to them all.

PERMISSIONS

Grateful acknowledgment is made to the following:

Robert Reich: Excerpts from *I'll Be Short: Essentials for a Decent Working Society*, by Robert Reich. Copyright © 2002 by Robert B. Reich. Reprinted by permission of the author and Beacon Press, Boston.

FOR THE CURIOUS ...
Source notes on the stories and data cited in this book are available online (www.tompeters.com/essentials/notes. php). Also on the Web are complete versions of the Cool Friends interviews excerpted in the book (www.tompeters. com/cool_friends/friends.php).

PICTURE CREDITS

Picture Researcher : Sarah Hopper
DK Picture Library : Richard Dabb

The publisher would like to thank the following for their kind permission to reproduce their photographs;
(Abbreviations key: t=top, b=below, r=right, l=left, c=centre, a=above, tl=top left, tr=top right, bl=below left, br=below right).

10: Corbis/Pete Saloutos; 15: Corbis/ Georgina Bowater (b); 20: Corbis/Matthias Kulka (tl); 23: Getty Images/The Image Bank (t); 24: Science Photo Library/Adam Hart-Davis (b); 26: Getty Images/Bob Scott; 32-3: Getty Images/Ian McKinnell; 38-39: Corbis/Hulton Deutsche Collection; 41: Getty Images; 42: Retna Pictures Ltd/Adrian Boot (b); 43: Getty Images; 45: Retna Pictures Ltd/Sara de Boer (c); 53: Corbis/Philip Harvey (t); 54-55: Corbis/James W.Porter; 57: Corbis; 59: Getty Images/David Gould (tr); 61: Getty Images/Yellow Dog Productions (tl), Getty Images/Jason Hetherington (tr), Getty Images/Paul Viant (bl), Getty Images/Peter Beavis (br); 66: Corbis/Pete Saloutos; 72-73: Getty Images/ Jean-Noel Reichel; 74: Getty Images/James Cotier; 77: Corbis/Andrew Brookes; 79: Corbis/Tim Pannell (t); 79: Getty Images/ David Buffington (b); 88-89: Getty Images/ James Balog; 94: Corbis/Pete Saloutos; 99: Corbis/Bob Daemmrich (tl), Corbis/Gregory Pace (tr), Corbis/Kim Kulish (bl); 99: Rex Features/BYX (br); 101: Corbis/Steve Prezant; 111: Corbis/Patrik Giardino; 118: Corbis/Pete Saloutos; 130-131: Corbis/Tim Davis; 132: Corbis/Helen King; 139: Getty Images/Jerry Driendl; 140: Corbis/Bettmann (b); 144: Corbis/Craig Hammell; 147: Corbis/ Randy Faris (t); 148-149: Mary Evans Picture Library; 152: Corbis/Jose Luis Pelaez (b); Corbis/LWA-Dann Tardif (t); Corbis/Steve Prezant (c); 157: Corbis/Mike Chew.

All other images © Dorling Kindersley. For further information see: www.dkimages.com

Hear Tom Peters Live with Red Audio (TM).

ABOUT THE AUTHOR

The Economist *called Tom Peters the Uber-guru.* BusinessWeek *labelled him "business's best friend and worst nightmare."* Fortune *tagged him as the Ur-guru of management, and compared him to Ralph Waldo Emerson, Henry David Thoreau, Walt Whitman, and H.L. Mencken. In an in-depth study released by Accenture's Institute for Strategic Change in 2002, he scored second among the top 50 "Business Intellectuals," behind Michael Porter and ahead of Peter Drucker.*

In 2004 the compilers of Movers and Shakers: The Brains and Bravado Behind Business *reviewed the contributions of 100 business thinkers and practitioners, from Machiavelli to J.P. Morgan to Jack Welch. Here's how the book summarized Tom's impact: "Tom Peters has probably done more than anyone else to shift the debate on management from the confines of boardrooms, academia, and consultancies to a broader, worldwide audience, where it has become the staple diet of the media and managers alike. Peter Drucker has written more and his ideas have withstood a longer test of time, but it is Peters—as consultant, writer, columnist, seminar lecturer, and stage performer—whose energy, style, influence, and ideas have shaped new management thinking."*

Tom's first book, coauthored with Robert J. Waterman, was In Search of Excellence *(1982). National Public Radio in 1999 placed the book among the "Top Three Business Books of the Century," and a poll by Bloomsbury Publishing in 2002 ranked it as the "greatest business book of all time." Tom followed* Search *with a string of international best-sellers:* A Passion for Excellence *(1985, with Nancy Austin),* Thriving on Chaos *(1987),* Liberation Management *(1992),* The Tom Peters Seminar: Crazy Times Call for Crazy Organizations *(1993),* The Pursuit of WOW! *(1994);* The Circle of Innovation: You Can't Shrink Your Way to Greatness *(1997), and a series of books on Reinventing Work—*The Brand You50, The Project50, *and* The Professional Service Firm50 *(1999). In 2003 Tom joined with publisher Dorling Kindersley to release* Re-imagine! Business Excellence in a Disruptive Age. *That book, which aims to reinvent the business book through energetic presentation of critical ideas, immediately became an international No.1 bestseller.*

Leadership guru Warren Bennis, the only person who knows both Tom and Peter Drucker first-hand, told a reporter, "If Peter Drucker invented modern management, Tom Peters vivified it." Indeed, throughout his career, Tom's overriding passion has been passion. Among his current passions: women as leaders; the supreme role of design in product and service differentiation; the creation of customer experiences that rival a Cirque du Soleil performance; and the enormous, underserved markets represented by women and by Boomers.

Born in Baltimore in 1942, Tom resided in Northern California from 1974 to 2000 and now lives on a 1,600-acre working farm in Vermont with his wife, Susan Sargent. He has degrees in civil engineering from Cornell University (B.C.E., M.C.E.) and in business from Stanford University (M.B.A., Ph.D.). He holds honorary doctorates from several institutions, including the State University of Management in Moscow (2004). Serving in the U.S. Navy from 1966 to 1970, he made two deployments to Vietnam (as a Navy Seabee) and survived a tour in the Pentagon. He also served as a senior White House drug-abuse advisor from 1973 to 1974. From 1974 to 1981, he worked at McKinsey & Co., becoming a partner and Organization Effectiveness practice leader in 1979. Tom is a Fellow of the International Academy of Management, the World Productivity Association, the International Customer Service Association, and the Society for Quality and Participation. Today, he presents about 75 major seminars each year (half of them outside the United States), and participates in numerous other learning events, both in person and on the Web.

SAY IT LOUD – THE ESSENTIALS MANIFESTO

They say...   I say...

They say...	I say...
Sure, we need "change."	We need REVOLUTION. NOW.
Your (my) language is extreme.	The times are extreme.
I am extreme.	I am a realist.
I demand too much.	"They" accept mediocrity too readily.
Brand You is not for everyone.	The alternative is unemployment.
Take a deep breath. Be calm.	Tell it to Wal*Mart. Tell it to China. Tell it to India. Tell it to Dell. Tell it to Microsoft.
What's wrong with a "good product"?	Wal*Mart or China or both are about to eat your lunch. Why can't you provide instead a Fabulous Experience?
The Web is a "useful tool."	The Web changes everything. Now.
We need an "initiative."	We need a Dream. And Dreamers.
Great Design is nice.	Great Design is mandatory.
You (I) overplay the "women's thing."	The minuscule share of Women in Senior Leadership Positions is a Waste and a Disgrace and a Strategic Marketing Error.
We need a "project" to explore "new markets."	We need Total Strategic Realignment to exploit the Women and Boomer markets.
"Wow" is "typical Tom."	"WOW" is a Minimum Survival Requirement.
We like people who, with steely determination, say, "I can make it better."	I love people who, with a certain maniacal gleam in their eye, perhaps even a giggle, say, "I can turn the world upside-down!"
Let's speed things up.	Let's transform the Corporate Metabolism until Insane Urgency becomes a Sacrament.
We want recruits with "spotless records."	Those "spots" are what defines Talent.
We favor a "team" that works in "harmony."	Give me a raucous brawl among the most creative people imaginable.
We want "happy" customers.	Give me pushy, needy, nasty, provocative customers who will drag me down Innovation Boulevard at 100mph.
We want to partner with "best of breed."	Give me Coolest of Breed.
Happy balance.	Creative Tension.
Peace, brother.	Bruise my feelings. Flatten my ego. SAVE MY JOB.
Plan it.	DO IT.
Market share.	Market Creation.
Basic black.	TECHNICOLOR RULES!
Conglomerate and Imitate.	Create and Innovate.
Improve and Maintain.	DESTROY and RE-IMAGINE!